creating CONFIDENCE

creating CONFIDENCE

How to develop your

PERSONAL POWER and **PRESENCE**

Meribeth Bunch

**KOGAN
PAGE**

First published in 1999
Reprinted in 1999

Kogan Page Limited
120 Pentonville Road
London N1 9JN

© Meribeth Bunch, 1999

The right of Meribeth Bunch to be identified as author of this work has been asserted by her in accordance with the Copyright, Design and Patents Act, 1988.

British Library Cataloguing in Publication Data
A CIP record for this book is available from the British Library.
ISBN 07494 2782 5

Typeset by Jean Cussons Typesetting, Diss, Norfolk
Printed and bound by Clays Ltd, St Ives plc

CONTENTS

Preface   9
Acknowledgements   11
Introduction   13

1. **Communication**   19
    Communication defined   20
    Balanced communication – body, voice, words   24
    The two most important concepts in personal
        communication   27
    Summary   30

2. **The self-critic, saboteur of change**   31
    The evolution of the self-critic   31
    Exercises   34

3. **Creating a positive presence – an overview**   35
    Developing personal space   36
    Potent invisible aspects   40
    Summary   45
    Observations and exercises   46

4. **Visibility and image: the physical and mental you**   **49**
    A note about confidence   49
    Physical alignment and its relationship to health,
        energy, image and voice   50
    Guidelines for checking and correcting posture   59
    Exercises   59

5. **Improve your voice**   **63**
    How the voice works: an overview   63
    Physical habits that interfere with voice and message   68
    Being expressive   71
    Summary: Working with your voice   62
    Exercises to improve voice and expression   75

6. **Listening and rapport**   **79**
    Listening   79
    Summary: The characteristics of skilled listeners   81
    Establishing rapport   82
    Exercises relating to listening and rapport   88

7. **Dealing with 'feedback' and criticism**   **91**
    Accepting criticism and suggestions   92
    Giving criticism or feedback   93
    Honesty with wisdom   95
    Giving effective feedback in group situations   96
    Personal guidelines for accepting and giving criticism   97

8. **The art of presentation**   **99**
    What makes a speaker interesting?   100
    Boredom factors in presentation   101
    Approaching presentation creatively   105
    Presentation tools   112

Contents

Interactive presentation and facilitation 114
A word about scientific or technical papers 116
Presentations as a part of a job interview 117
Timing your talk 117
Giving your presentation 118
What if ...? 121
Summary 127

9. **Action planning and summary** **129**
Action planning 129
Summary 131
Ways of maintaining your personal power 131
Using these tools wisely 132

Further reading *135*

PREFACE

The concepts and ideas in this book have come from working with students and professionals in business, the performing arts and science and from my own personal experience of learning things the hard way. Most of my clients come to me asking for more confidence. We work on presence and personal power and their perceptions about those things and they leave with confidence. Confidence is an end-product that comes from many small accomplishments and the courage to take personal risks. To my knowledge there are no pills for confidence.

I have observed people physically shrink in front of my eyes when performing, speaking, or holding conversations with people or audiences they perceived to be important. These moments of shrinking are times when personal power has been given away. In each instance, it was not known or understood that presence and personal power are inside us, not in someone else's hands. Once we have the opportunity to learn about and correct personal habits that cause us to give these things away, we begin to stop the process of damaging our self-esteem and confidence.

It takes some time to realize the patterns of behaviour and thought that contribute to the shrinkage. At first, we usually recognize the pattern after it has happened. Later we realize it while we are in the middle of it. Finally, after many difficult lessons, we spot it before it can happen. I relate this to slipping on a banana skin and call it the 'banana skins of life'. It is easy to slide into patterns over and over again because we have not recognized the signals early enough to stop. Once you slip there is no way to stop until you have gone the length of the skin. It is only when we become aware of what is in our path that we find a way to avoid it.

It is important for each of us to maintain our personal power and integrity. When we give them away, confidence and self-esteem go as well. Some ways of maintaining personal power and integrity are outlined in this book. They have been tried and tested by me over the last 30 years in my teaching and consulting. By helping people gain new perspectives and reasons to release old perceptions and patterns of behaviour, they are enabled to be themselves in the best sense, and in turn, allow the same in others.

Choosing for yourself is enabling. Following teachings, rules and dogmas blindly can lead to loss of personal power. This includes our own private dogmas as well. The dictator within can do a fine job of creating them. Personal power is about bringing out and evolving the excellent inner leader in all of us. It is not about authority, aggression or assertiveness but the joy of personal discovery and choosing positive and gratifying change.

We rarely take on anything unless we can see it for ourselves. While new ideas might be accepted intellectually, putting them into practice requires taking personal risks. Once we have a chance to try out new ideas practically, we can then weigh the options and choose what is most useful at the moment. This book offers new perspectives, suggestions for taking small, non-threatening risks and many options for thought, experimentation and change.

Enjoy the journey.

Meribeth Bunch, Ph.D.
London
November 1998

Acknowledgements

The experiences of trial and error and learning the hard way have contributed hugely to this book. Therefore I want to thank first those people who, over the course of my life, I have perceived to have made my life difficult. I learnt positive, valuable lessons. Thank you.

There are others who have nurtured and supported me in my quest to learn, grow and understand about myself and my own power. The early and ongoing support from Trudy Sanford has been valued over many years. My thanks also go to Betty Gould, Vivien Gill (no longer physically present) and Sue Minns. My particular thanks to Dadi Janki, a woman of great wisdom, to Jane Vukovic, a fairy godmother to myself and many others, and my sister, Susanne Nohlgren, who has offered steadfast encouragement.

I am grateful to Simon Pearsall, a very clever cartoonist. He has added the spice to this book. My thanks also to Bruce Abrahams and John Chapman for their careful reading of the manuscript and, finally, to Janice Chapman for our long discussions about the voice, and life and learning in general.

*This book is dedicated to those who dare
to make the best of themselves*

Introduction

Going with the flow today means that it is necessary to live in the chaos that looks set to remain with us for some time to come. How well and how comfortably we live with this is a sign of our inner strength, self-esteem and confidence. Most of us maintain the hope that we will find a way to control chaos only to find ourselves squarely in the middle of a whirlwind. Those without confidence and an inner source of strength to deal with chaos are soon left behind, discouraged or stressed out. It does not have to be so. With appropriate tools everyone is capable of developing a physical, mental and spiritual presence which in turn leads to increased confidence, understanding and the effective and integral use of personal power.

Personal power, as discussed in this book, implies the following:

❏ having an innate sense of yourself that is not dependent on what you think other people think;
❏ the ability and confidence to find out or ask what you need to know to do your job or task well;
❏ the ability to listen to comments and criticism and pursue them positively until a way is found to resolve the situation with integrity and without emotional attachment to the outcome;
❏ and finally, to take care of your own needs. In doing so, you are far better able to maintain your energy and sense of self-worth and you will be free to share and to give others what they may need at the time.

Perception and self image

Very few people have personal power imbued as a gift from birth. We grow up with an infinite variety of perceptions, belief systems and misconceptions about ourselves and others. As we grow and mix with others socially and at work, these patterns and attitudes manifest themselves and can easily throw us into turmoil because we are not centred. We are at odds with the working atmosphere and ourselves, and stress is the inevitable result.

The business community has begun to recognize employee stress and to make strides to help. Counsellors, massage therapists, other personal therapies, even gyms are being added to the working environment. However, these are cosmetic unless that environment is pleasant, energizing and supportive – even fun.

Over the past 35 years I have had the privilege of working with executives, managers and sales staff in large and small businesses, charities, university students and faculty and those in the performing arts. In my capacity as a consultant I have noted a number of patterns that present themselves in the professional arena:

1. *We make hard work of work.*

There is a perception that 'one must behave differently at work'. We leave a comfortable home environment where we speak and interact easily and naturally, where we are natural hosts and hostesses dealing with others sensitively and with an awareness of what is happening around us. However, in a situation that we think is professional or work related, we resort to a behaviour based on perceptions about business, inadequate role models, some from academic, military or dictatorial home environments, and lack of training in basic communication skills. We fall into the trap of playing a role rather than being ourselves and then try to create something artificial to match our perceptions of how we 'should' be. This results in staff and professionals who are tired, stressed and lacking in self-esteem and confidence because there is no inner power. It has been given away to those people perceived to be strong, superior to, or to be in control of their lives in some way.

When perceptions are distorted, it is easy to lose the ability to be ourselves and stand up for our own values. We become mentally and emotionally occupied with our own perceptions of what we think others are thinking of us and lose clarity of focus. Situations are replayed in the mind while we shrink into the nearest chair or the woodwork to go over what we would like to have said and done. Personal power has been given away and the groundwork for an atmosphere of distrust and secret grievances has been laid.

2. Basic communication and rapport skills can be taught and have been neglected.

While companies are beginning to train management levels in this area, very little is being done about it at staff levels. Few staff are given adequate communication skills training at induction. It is either assumed that those skills are in place already or that they are reserved for management development programmes. Companies including such training at induction provide adequate communication tools with which to interact effectively and thereby enable their staff to interact with the public at an advantage.

3. Being 'me' is an important starting point for good communication skills.

In my work with people in business, I have found that when people leave home, they perceive the need to play a role, or be something 'other'. It is very difficult to put a group of people playing roles together and, at the same time, create an effective and efficient workforce. Our perceptions are often skewed. How we look and act, and how we *think* we look and act, are very different.

4. *The words 'mentor' or facilitator perhaps are more appropriate than manager.*

I've often said to managers, 'If you want to know how you behave, look at those under you because they will behave like you. They want your job and see your example as one to follow.' Those people, in any walk of life, who are nurtured as human beings, thrive and are helped to gain in confidence and self-esteem. Managers who nurture create future executives who will do the same.

5. *Staff are asked to change without being given any specific tools with which to implement the change.*

During periodic assessments staff hear such general comments as, 'Your teamwork needs improving' or 'You need to be better at communication'. I believe that each person does his or her best with the personal tools he or she has at any given time. Until we know what needs to be altered and specifically *how* to do it, it is virtually impossible to implement the change. A person with reasonable self-esteem will have the presence of mind to ask questions or do some detective work to produce specific ways of sorting out the problem. Questions that elicit useful responses are the most useful. For example, 'Tell me what area of my teamwork is a problem', 'In regard to my communication – is it my words, my attitudes, my expression, etc that need attention?' Having the presence of mind to ask questions when seeming criticism is being thrown your way creates difficulties for vulnerable staff. Many people are too mortified to ask and are left to their own devices to sort out the problem.

6. *When you want to reach someone quickly, show him or her a relevant picture.*

Most of the books written for the business community are full of words, are very serious and tend to have few or no pictures or cartoons. Studies have shown that the majority of the population store their information in mental pictures. The old adage, 'A picture is worth a thousand words', is still true.

7. *Presentations tend to be based on models of school essays or theses that are meant to be read – not spoken.*

This is interesting because more than 75 per cent of communication is considered to be non-verbal.

As we move into the 21st century, professional men and women need specific and practical tools for communication skills and personal development. These tools can be made more accessible by being presented in a light, readable, user-friendly manner with pertinent illustrations. It is the intention of this book to do that.

OBJECTIVES

❏ To offer guidelines for developing a positive personal presence that contribute to a healthy, vibrant person and ultimately a positive climate in which to work.

❏ To treat communication and presentation skills as basic to presence and confidence and therefore firmly placed at the heart of personal growth rather than peripheral to it.

❏ To offer appropriate tools and language for individuals to find a way to strengthen or regain their personal power and confidence in a variety of situations.

1

COMMUNICATION

Learning to communicate effectively is a lifelong process. Often it is a combination of trial and error and learning the hard way. This process contributes – sometimes positively and at other times negatively – to perceptions of ourselves and others. Patterns and habits of communication develop from childhood and are carried well into adulthood and old age. These habits are so subconscious that much of the time we have no realistic idea of how we are perceived by others.

People communicate in the best way they know and do not realize when and how they are failing to convey their intended message. When it is understood that the message is not clear, it is not a matter of blaming the past or making excuses; rather, it involves the maturity to recognize and change the elements of your communication that are not serving you well for those that are more effective. It is a matter of saying or thinking:

❏ 'No matter what has happened in the past, do I want this pattern of behaviour now?'
❏ 'It is my choice to behave, react, respond differently and now I choose to do it another way'.
❏ 'Past is past; I cannot go on behaving the way I have in the past and expect anything other than the responses I evoked in the past'.

There is a saying, 'When you think the way you have always thought, you will act the way you have always acted and you will get what you have always got'.

COMMUNICATION DEFINED

The word, communication, in itself tells a story. It is derived from the Latin word *communis* meaning common. Some other words derived from this root are community, communion and communitarian. We communicate by creating common ground with those to whom we speak. When that is established, a sense of community is begun and then followed by something greater than the whole; a spirit of community, which by some might be termed a kind of communion. The result of community spirit is the fostering and nurturing of people who co-operate, form effective teams, become friends and can be called communitarians.

Developing a sense of community is important in the day-to-day running of a business. This is difficult when business executives today are in so many meetings that there is barely time for deskwork. These sessions consist of everything from one-to-one discussions to committee meetings. It might be said that a typical executive day consists of wall-to-wall people, talking, brainstorming, organizing and facilitating. Those with good communication skills and an understanding of the importance of the business community soon develop a rapport with their colleagues. This fosters and creates a pleasant atmosphere where support and a sense of ease and co-operation are predominant. The result is good team-building and a focus on the projects and aims of the day rather than personal issues that arise because there is a perceived lack of support or dialogue.

There are several common scenarios that are prevalent:

FIRST THE IDEAL

A give–give situation where each person is dedicated to fulfilling his role as defined by the project. Each team member is fully focused on giving his or her best to the goals of the project. Here the attention and language used is project-oriented and based on fulfilling what is needed to accomplish it. In this situation there are likely to be dialogues like the following:

A: 'I am feeling pushed and would like some help with this report.'
B: 'What's the biggest problem? Do you need secretarial help or another mind/brain to help you think through it?'
A: 'I would like an additional mind on this.'
B: 'OK, I will ask Sue if she would be willing to help and get back to you today.'

Rather than a commonly encountered situation like the one below:

B: 'Why isn't that report in yet? Are you sure you are up to this job?'
A: 'I'm sorry, if Joe had got his work in on time, I might have finished it by now.'

Note that the first conversation is open and honest rather than using excuses or blame. However, in the second conversation, there are two negative factors at play. Firstly, the question is accusative and finger-pointing. It is difficult not to be threatened by this approach. However, no matter what the reason, the report is not done. It is important to acknowledge that fact. Then the conversation is directed towards the report and not anyone's shortcomings. Secondly, apportioning blame does nothing towards getting the report done. How can the project go ahead if A is busy putting blame on someone else? When the focus of the conversation is related to the project itself, you are better able to avoid personal issues and less likely to create the need for excuses. Every time someone feels the need to make excuses, his or her confidence levels sink a little.

SECOND SCENARIO: THE 'ENERGY DRAINER'

Practically everyone can tell you about knowing someone who, when in their presence, seems to makes them feel tired. These people are unknowingly draining the energy that you are unwittingly giving away.

Often these 'drainers' are the 'poor me' types – the ones that seem to need constant bolstering. Working with such people can be time-consuming. However, it is important for the project or job that they pull their own weight and feel valued as team members. Ideally, you will find some areas of the project where they feel they can contribute what they do best with confidence. When this is not the case, you may have to consider placing this person in another area.

It is useful to have an armoury of questions such as:
'Where, in this project/job, do you feel you most comfortable in using your skills?'
'Would you like help writing the report?'
'Could I ask you to be in charge of ...?'(This does not have to be a major job – just a small responsibility.)

Finally, when the person is unable to take any responsibility for themselves, you have a problem and you will have to give them an assignment. If they do not like it, they have only themselves to blame. You have done your best.

The third scenario is very familiar in business today. This involves the 'giver' who does not ask, but rather sees another's needs and orders change or presents an 'unwanted gift'. Anyone who has ever taught or been a boss will recognize this. It is difficult not to help when you perceive another person's need or when you are particularly enthusiastic about something. However, when that person has not asked for what you are offering or there has been no prior consultation, they may be offended by being given it. It may make them feel inadequate.

When the ground for the offering is not carefully prepared, the following perceptions may be encountered:

Giver:

'I give him everything and he is never grateful.'
'He has had so many chances to make changes and has not taken any of them.'

Receiver:

'My boss never understands me.'
'She asks me to go on courses at the most inconvenient times.'
'I do not know why I need to learn more about ...'
'No one has said I was lacking in that area.'

Rather than issuing what is perceived to be an order, spend time piquing the employee's interest and helping her to see and appreciate her own needs. Ideally, the 'gift' is then presented after it has been requested. By approaching others' perceived needs carefully with sensitivity and understanding, you gain their trust and are better able to have open and honest discussions with them.

Asking appropriate questions allows others to tell you what they want and need and is vitally important for an effective and efficient working team. This enables everyone to take responsibility for themselves. Such sensitivity to another human being is critical to developing a good working relationship and contributes greatly to that person's sense of confidence and self-esteem. It is too easy to think that the quickest way forward is to issue an order – yes, in conditions of war this may be important. However, in the professional environment, dedication and loyalty come from a different set of techniques and values.

BALANCED COMMUNICATION – BODY, VOICE, WORDS

If you have ever wondered how other people misinterpret your message – here is the answer. Your message is out of balance. When your body, voice and words do not agree completely, it causes doubt in the mind of the listener. No matter how well intended your words, when your voice, unintentional habits, or even clothes, are not in balance with the message, your words are going to be lacking conviction.

Research (Argyle *et al*, 1970) has shown that the impression you make on others is comprised of three areas:

1. that which is visible – your face and eyes, gestures, physical habits, clothes, etc;
2. your voice – the quality, tone, pitch, rhythm and speed;
3. the actual words.

The study found that words are only 7 per cent of the communication, voice is 38 per cent and the visual aspects are 55 per cent.

Obviously these figures relate to person-to-person communication. Imagine the additional importance of the voice when talking on the phone.

When my clients are first confronted with the statistics relating to this, they moan and offer many different reasons why the statistics are really different – until they see themselves on video. Then the realization sinks in. Their perceptions and the reality are different. They then work in a much more efficient way to convey their messages. What seemed to them to be over-the-top was more effective and their old pattern was then judged by themselves to be lacking in conviction.

While it is easy to become caught up in these figures, the important concept here is *balance*. This does not mean that you need to cut out 93 per cent of your words (some might), but rather, what you say has to look and sound like the words you are using. For example, to say with a smile on your face that you do not want to do something, sends a double message and creates a question in the mind of the listener – no matter how much you think you mean the words. The rationale for the smile might be something like 'I did not want to offend him'. This is a problem of faulty perception and creates doubts in the mind of the listener.

Another example seen in presentations relates to using the hands. Too often a presenter has been told to keep her hands

A NOTE ABOUT HANDS...

quiet and stop waving them about. However, most of us use our hands quite naturally and expressively in casual, comfortable situations – when we do not think we are giving a presentation. In presentations people tend to develop a twitch or a movement pattern that replaces the natural use of their hands. In other words, they will twitch at the moment they would normally have used their hands for expressive purposes – or at times when they want to emphasize a word. These movements rarely have anything to do with the meaning of the words and interfere with the clarity of the message. This issue will be discussed in detail in a later chapter.

A final example relates to voice quality. It is not uncommon to hear someone asking others to be calm or confident with a voice that is full of tension and is of poor quality. Something does not fit. That person has no idea that his voice sounds harsh or is offensive. How the voice is heard inside our heads and how it sounds to the listener is very different. Anyone who hears his voice on tape for the first time will attest to that. Tensions and erroneous perceptions of the quality in the voice again unintentionally confuse the message.

Interestingly, most people spend about 98 per cent of their time conscientiously working on the words – not realizing the importance of preparing voice and body. Add a few nerves to that lack of complete preparation and you have a lost message. You can never assume that it is the responsibility of the listener to get your message. It is your job to make it as easy as possible for anyone hearing you. The more difficult it is for your audience, the more of the message is lost.

It is easy to assume that the burden of responsibility is on the listener to absorb everything. This is largely because our learning styles have been dictated by schooling that insists on our taking in copious amounts of material – often presented badly.

Business and social situations are not the same as our days in school. People do not need to have to work hard to listen and get the message. When we speak, we must command attention by the clarity of our visual signals, voice, emotional honesty and text of our messages. It is the responsibility of each of us to help people listen by giving out such congruent signals. Balancing the message means we have to be self-aware, sensitive to the response of others, willing to change faulty perceptions of ourselves and others and able to listen without an ongoing internal conversation.

THE TWO MOST IMPORTANT CONCEPTS IN PERSONAL COMMUNICATION

I want to be here

The most important aspect of any communication lies in one critically important attitude. It is simply this: *I want to be here!* The implication of this statement is enormous. It means being fully present with mind and body fully attentive to what is going on. When you want to be here you consider what you are doing at the moment to be the most important thing there is.

Think about it: there is no other place you can be except where you are at this minute. Wishing and hoping that you were somewhere else simply takes your mind and attention away from the present moment. There are whole committee meetings where most of the members are mentally on holiday. Virtually nothing is accomplished and another meeting is called to finish the work. Functioning in the present is the only way to accomplish the task at hand and it is certainly the only way for you to be heard by another person. Being completely 'here' is the first step to speaking, listening and to developing a recognizable sense of presence.

Acknowledging others

When you want to be where you are, you will also want to be aware of those around you. The second most important concept in communication is acknowledging other people. I have never met a person who did not need acknowledgement. We all need it. It is part of human validation and the nourishment process.

CASE STUDY

While teaching a customer service course in a large company, I found that the young, shy staff did not like saying, 'Can I help you?' My response was to give them a list of ways to acknowledge customers differently. Speaking or a greeting of some sort is the most obvious way to recognize someone. However, for those who are shy or those who have been taught not to speak to strangers, this can be difficult. There are a number of alternatives: smile, think the positive greeting you might have spoken or make a friendly gesture or nod of the head that will let them know they have been seen. I have seen customers and other staff seemingly ignored by someone talking on the phone. Even when you are busy, the other person needs to know that you realize they are there. Many staff are unknowingly rude to customers when they do not acknowledge their presence because they are not ready to wait on them.

CASE STUDY

James, a young executive, felt his boss was asking him to do something he thought was unnecessary. His boss wanted a listed summary of his activities. James did not think it was necessary because he saw no need for it. He felt his boss was just being overly exacting. When I asked James what his boss's strengths were, he listed an ability with detail as one of them. Yet, that ability was being partly denied him by James. I asked James if he had the detail wanted. He said yes, it was on his computer. I then asked if his secretary had access to that information. Again the answer was yes. The next question was, 'Do you feel comfortable asking her to compile these details for a once-a-week meeting with your boss?' The answer was yes.

Once James understood that he was continually denying one of the strengths of his boss, he realized why his relationship with him was poor. We need to find a way to bypass our own opinions and judgements so that we are able to acknowledge the strengths of other people. Unless we can do that, they will feel uncomfortable and unappreciated for what they do well. This form of acknowledgement is vital for any kind of relationship.

No one likes being ignored or feeling like they have been over-looked. The easiest way to acknowledge another person is to see them and let them know they have been seen.

Another area of acknowledgement that is neglected or not understood is how we honour the people around us in a profes-sional or social context. People must be honoured for what they do best and for their preferences, not for what we think they should be doing or thinking. Too often it is easy to dismiss what someone else desires because we ourselves do not think it is necessary. How are we to know that?

SUMMARY

Your appreciation of your friends and colleagues will show in your recognition and acknowledgement of them. When you determine to want to be where you are at all times, you will begin to enjoy everything and everyone in your space. It then becomes easy to establish the common ground necessary for good communication.

2

THE SELF-CRITIC, SABOTEUR OF CHANGE

THE EVOLUTION OF THE SELF-CRITIC

Your own criticism is the great saboteur of change. The biggest obstacle to personal growth, communication and certainly presentation of all kinds, is the self-critic. It is like an alien that takes us over, determines the words we use, the actions we take and contributes to a general state of fear or panic.

We come by it naturally. Many methods of education use criticism as a tool for teaching. All of us have grown up with this method, as have the generations before us. The result is generations of people who have an internal radio that constantly tells them how bad they are at what they do, destroys self-respect and confidence and creates critics who do the same to everyone else.

The origins of the self-critic stem from a common set of vocabulary used since time immemorial and ingrained in us from parents, teachers and friends. (This is not about blame, it is about a long tradition. None of these people deliberately set about to cause the problem. It was the only way they knew.) There are three pairs of these words. They are:

right–wrong

should–ought

control–hold

Think about it. When someone tells you that you have to get something 'right', your first reaction is to become tense or to worry. When we think we have to get something right, we are put at a disadvantage immediately and begin to doubt our own ability to do it.

Even in role-plays, telling someone that they have done something wrong causes them to go pale. Kinesiology tests and studies in psycho-neuro-immunology (PNI) suggest that using these words causes a temporary depletion of the immune system.

Once we have been told we have to get it right or that we have got it wrong, our defence mechanisms begin to respond by creating excuses or internalizing the criticism. Those who have levelled the criticism begin to tell us what we should or ought to have done. Our minds do the same. Now we have a double-barrelled situation where the rights and wrongs and the shoulds and oughts are competing for our thinking time. When the words should and ought are used, a person can feel talked at or preached to.

Once we have been chastised because something was not right and told what we should have done, we begin to think of ways to control the situation. That is where the defensiveness, denials and blame begin. We want to hold on and control what is happening and what is being said. Soon this internal dialogue of criticism, judgement and blame begins to take over situations in which we are concerned or deem important. In doing so we stifle spontaneity, creativity and intuition – the very things we need most. While most people admire these qualities in others, they are reticent to let go of control long enough to find out what being spontaneous, creative and intuitive is like. It seems too risky. Sometimes we have to lose control to gain freedom.

This is particularly true in presentations, interviews, competitive sport and performance. Sportsmen and women will attest to the times when their bodies were shut out because of too much mental discussion. This made them stiff and unable to respond to the situation. When this inner conversation with the self-critic is present, you exhibit a stilted, monotonous voice, a rigid body and eyes that are not seeing. In other words the person speaking or performing is not present – only the self-critic.

I had a long talk with my self-critic and we made two agreements. The first one is, 'My self-critic may not talk to me while I am talking or writing. We can confer afterwards when necessary'. The second, and more difficult is, 'My self-critic may not give its opinion unless I ask for it. Sometimes I have to mentally put it in a box outside the door so it will stop interfering'.

Of course, there are times when it is appropriate to analyse what we are doing. Then the self-critic can be invited to help. However any analysis while something is in progress stops the process dead or slows it to a stuttering crawl. Creativity and change need a mind that is free of vocabulary such as right–wrong, should–ought and control–hold. This vocabulary is what the rampant self-critic uses to become stagnant.

EXERCISES

1.   Go through any recent material you have written and change the words right–wrong, should–ought and control–hold to less dictatorial and finger-pointing vocabulary.

An example: We have got to get this contract right.
Change to: It is important to do quality work on this contract.

2.   Test yourself by going a whole day without using the above words in conversation. What happens? What other words and phrases can you use instead?

3

CREATING A POSITIVE PRESENCE – AN OVERVIEW

Presence is obtainable. It is a matter of knowing what it is and working at it. Often presence is confused with the term 'charisma'. A person with charisma has achieved a special way of being that seems to permeate both him or herself and the room. Some people are born with it and for others it is the end-product of dedicated inner personal and spiritual work. Presence has to do with a sense of space and how to use it. Anyone with a desire to change and a little imagination can achieve presence.

CASE STUDY

In my seminars I ask the question, 'How much space are you occupying at this moment?' The majority reply with something like, 'Just around my chair', 'A direct line to you', or 'As far as the person sitting next to me'. I then ask the group to ascertain the amount of space I am occupying. Without hesitation, the response is, 'The whole room'. The next question is, 'How do you know?' Answers I get to this question include, 'Something about your posture', 'You are standing and we are sitting', 'You are in charge of this seminar, etc'. They know when someone is commanding space, yet cannot quite discern the specific reasons why.

DEVELOPING PERSONAL SPACE

Why do you take notice when some people enter a room? How is it that you know when friends are happy or sad without speaking to them? How do you know which days not to disturb the boss? These are things we sense or feel – often without knowing the reason intellectually.

Your personal space is your energy field – a portable 'home', if you wish – and is comprised of many facets. If those around us can discern it, it must be more than just imagination. A person's presence and that individual's use of personal space have a number of visible and invisible factors which contribute to the whole picture.

The obvious indicators of a person's presence are posture, energy and health, the eyes, the voice and levels of awareness and sensitivity. The seemingly invisible factors such as attitudes, thoughts and imagination contribute equally. In the end, the whole is greater than the sum of its parts. However, by looking at the parts we can begin to analyse presence and then create ways of gaining it.

Posture – static or dynamic?

Physical alignment and posture contribute enormously to presence and are crucial to commanding space. Balanced alignment and good posture help us to look energetic and healthy, and contribute to voice quality and the kind of image we convey.

Postural bad habits begin early. However, they are correctable as long as you are willing to cope with feeling strange for a week or two. (As you know, change always creates a feeling of not being in our habitual comfort zone.) It is important to remember that the body is full of atoms that vibrate. Therefore posture is dynamic, not static. Unfortunately, the word itself tends to be perceived as something rigid or fixed. It would be preferable for you to think of yourself being as flexible, mobile and as physically responsive as a cat. When we think of ourselves as having such a dynamic flexibility, it brings energy and flow to body, voice and image. Those with this kind of energy have sparkling, alive eyes, look healthy and vibrant and appear to be a person you would like to know better.

The eyes – just looking or really seeing?

Nothing is more attractive than a person with shining, sparkling, fully present eyes. Such eyes are an indication of the expansiveness of your space and interest in 'being here'. Eyes with a light in them show life, energy, awareness and a reflection of a physically, mentally and spiritually healthy person. Your eyes hold the key to a large amount of information about you. They have served as a basis for diagnosis of physical and mental problems by different therapies and systems of medicine for centuries. Sayings like, 'The eyes are the mirror of the soul' permeate the literature. Many love affairs have begun because of being drawn to someone's eyes and many poems have been written to this effect.

It is easy to ascertain the presence of a person by the eyes. When you have eyes that are seeing, you are fully present in the moment and ready to listen or respond. Eyes that reflect thinking, feeling or inner listening are not seeing but appear to be defocused or roaming inwardly. This can happen when we are thinking about something, looking for an answer or pre-occupied with our own internal dialogues and feelings. For example, watch a speaker who is self-conscious. No doubt the eyes are not really present in the room and neither is the message because it has been forgotten. It is obvious that the speaker is thinking of him or herself rather than what is being discussed. When you are 'self-centred', you prevent yourself from being fully present and it is most apparent in your eyes.

The most widely used – and abused – term related to using the eyes is 'eye contact'. Rarely is this concept defined adequately. Most of us have been left to our own devices when figuring out how to do it. Too often eye contact becomes 'eyeball' gazing and it is extremely uncomfortable for all parties.

Many presenters have been taught to choose one member of an audience to whom to direct their message. This kind of attention creates a number of problems, especially for the poor person picked to be *the* one. The 'one' chosen has to remain glued to the speaker – he or she cannot escape this constant gaze. Secondly, the rest of the audience is then neglected, and nine times out of ten they feel left out of the talk or conversation. The presenter who uses such a technique limits the scope of his or her presence considerably.

How you see people is extremely important to the way you are perceived by them and is an indication of the way you are managing your personal space. When you use 180-degree vision or a wide peripheral vision to see another person, they know they have been seen and you have given them a very powerful form of acknowledgement. No one likes to feel ignored. Having tunnel vision when around people, whether it is simply a bad habit or deliberate, can be interpreted as being cold, aloof and uncaring towards your fellow human beings. Everyone needs acknowledgement and the simple gesture of seeing them is the easiest way to show it.

Seeing and looking are two different things. Looking tends to be a bit tunnel-visioned. Seeing involves the use of our peripheral vision – the vision that we use when we do not want to miss anything that is happening. Classroom teachers use this all the time. They want to know what children all over the whole room are doing. They have been accused of having eyes in the back of their heads. You need that same vision and awareness in order to know how your audience is responding, whether they are asleep or need a change of pace or energy. This kind of visual awareness is important and keeps you present.

Peripheral vision involves using a broad scope of seeing and involves using 180-degree vision. Most of us are physically capable of achieving nearly 180 degrees of vision. You can test this for yourself by extending your arms to the front with your hands touching. While looking straight ahead, move your arms slowly apart, keeping them at shoulder level. Note the point where you can no longer see both hands. It is probably close to 180 degrees. Without moving your head you can see the ceiling, the floor, everything within the 180 degrees in detail. You are seeing in the context of the whole.

When you look at another person this way, you see that person and most of the adjacent surroundings at the same time. This is very different to intently glaring into their eyes and being unaware of what else may be in your space.

Instead, you are visually aware of the whole scene and your eyes portray a softer, less aggressive look, as if the eyes are placed further back in the skull. Those who glare tend to look as if their eyeballs are bulging. Such a gaze is intimidating and uncomfortable.

Awareness

Once you begin to see with a wider vision, your sensitivity is heightened. You are alert to your audience, yourself, and your environment and well on your way to 360-degree awareness. This heightened awareness increases your sensitivity to those around you, sounds, colours, smells and the quality of the air. You are alert and kept in the present by the millions of antennae around your body that constantly feed you information.

POTENT INVISIBLE ASPECTS

Sometimes it is the invisible rather than the visible attributes of a person that define them more precisely. The obvious aspects of presence have been introduced above. However, what is sensed and felt about a person contributes equally to personal space and presence. You may think that these factors are difficult to define, change or improve. However, it is precisely these areas that we redefine continually as we pursue inner growth and development. These include such things as thought patterns, attitudes, belief systems, our sense of imagination, play and our ability to change our inner processes to adapt to current situations. Such factors are critical to personal survival today.

Thoughts

Learning to live with overly active internal conversations is not easy. However, such over-activity puts invisible busy signs on us and inhibits our presence. Your thought patterns are more visible than you think (just ask someone who knows you well). There are many meditation and mind-control courses and systems that devote themselves full time to teaching people to practise a modicum of control over their thought processes.

An inner stillness is requisite to making clear, informed decisions about every part of your life. Thoughts are much like the chatter of a very active internal radio. When we are occupied completely in our own minds, it is virtually impossible to be observant or listen. Being fully present demands a mind that has space to see, listen and observe. Needed answers can be found with a quiet mind.

The person who has mainly positive thoughts is much easier to be around than someone who is occupied with ongoing internal critical conversation. The positive person fills his or her space with a pleasant atmosphere. Most of us like to be around such people. On the other hand, when you have an over-abundance of negative thoughts, you give out a prickly atmosphere and quickly send people away or make them wonder why they came to see you in the first place.

Attitudes

Thought patterns that are reinforced over a long period of time become the attitudes and belief systems with which we lead our lives. We grow up with attitudes derived from the positive and negative experience gained from family, cultural and educational environments and the 'school of hard knocks'. Being objective is easy to talk about, difficult to achieve. We all carry a full suitcase of attitudes and preconceived ideas of how we need to function in a variety of situations.

Having a positive attitude is not only an asset, it expands your presence. For anyone to have a comfortable space for themselves and others, a positive attitude is essential. Those who do not have this, and insist on being continual pessimists, drag down the energy of everyone around them. Having a positive attitude does not mean that nothing negative ever happens. It simply means that you have the energy and ability to deal with negativity or unpleasantness in a mature, responsible manner.

'I want to be here' is an example of a positive attitude. By living this statement you create an atmosphere that encourages openness, sharing, honest discourse – and most of all an expanded and compelling energy field. On a subconscious level, others are generally aware of your attitude. It affects them and the rest of the environment. Think of it this way – if you put a drop of red paint into a whole bucket of white paint, it will still come out pink. It is the same with thoughts – they can turn the atmosphere blue!

Imagination

Preconceived ideas about work often cause us to ignore our most creative and imaginative thoughts. The most neglected gift we have is that of our imagination. It is the aspect we tend to deem unimportant at work and leave at home with the children. What ever happened to the statement, 'All work and no play makes Jack a dull boy'? Ask yourself why work, by definition, can be considered dull or boring. We spend most of the hours of our adult lives doing what we call work. What miserable human beings we can be without using our imaginative and creative resources in our professions – no matter how serious the responsibility. Who said that we could not mix work and pleasure? If you have perceived these two things to be incompatible, ask yourself why and do at least one imaginative thing immediately. Imagination stimulates creativity, curiosity and a sense of play. Those who can enjoy this aspect of themselves are more likely to be able to laugh with others and at themselves, are happy in their jobs and succeed in achieving desired goals with ease.

Visualization

Imagination taken one step further becomes visualization. It is an extremely potent tool. Visualization is your ability to picture yourself in or project yourself into a situation. It is a way of creating your space, programming positive thoughts, creating confidence in a variety of situations and, in general, programming your mind and body to achieve what you want.

Many top sports personalities speak of this kind of training as being critical to their performance. Just as they see themselves winning, having stamina and doing well, you can do the same in your personal and professional life. It is a good way to prepare for important presentations, meetings, interviews and public performance. Musicians are learning to use this to enable them to be more confident and to use their nervous energy in a positive way while performing.

Visualization is your way of creating an environment where you are able to do your best. It has nothing to do with having power or the advantage over another person. For example, in an interview situation, you desire to do your best – and you also wish to explore the situation and get to know the other people. In the final analysis, you may not want the position. However, you need the presence of mind to discover whether this is the place for you. By visualizing yourself being at ease and asking appropriate questions, you will create that possibility in your mind and it is likely to happen. In some ways it is similar to programming your computer. When you are busy visualizing yourself being nervous, inept and hoping to do well, you are setting yourself up for a possible negative outcome. You want to create an atmosphere in which you have options as to how you behave and react rather than becoming caught up in old patterns that are unhelpful.

Genetic and cultural factors

In the best of all worlds, we retain the positive aspects of what we inherit genetically and culturally. These can include a disposition towards longevity and good health, a good physical structure, a pleasant voice or such things as regional and family speech patterns. They are all to be honoured and savoured as part of your unique inheritance.

The unique self

You may give this part of yourself many names – 'persona', soul, etc. I describe this part as your core, the spirit that lives in you that no one else has. It is the very thing that makes you human.

SUMMARY

The expanded human

Your space is an energy field that can be expanded and contracted at will. You are in charge of it. You can choose to want to be where you are, stand tall, acknowledge those around you, see rather than look, think positive thoughts about someone, use your imagination and visualize yourself being able to do these things. It is possible to do this at any time and anywhere. When you are brave enough to do these things as part of daily life, the atmosphere in which you work changes – becoming more congenial, comfortable and less stressed. Negotiations and difficult decisions are treated differently, with the focus directed towards the task at hand rather than personal issues.

It took a long time for me to realize the phrase 'human being' was not one word and that the second word was a verb. 'Being' creates a comfortable home that can expand at will to accommodate a variety of physical, mental and emotional states. Think of this home as one that is portable and expandable and it goes everywhere with you. It is much like your house. However, it is your personal space that can include whoever you choose.

Our behaviour changes when we feel at home. For example,

when friends or strangers have been invited into your home you become the gracious host or hostess. You are aware of the needs of your guests, or if there is anyone who looks as if your attention is required. You introduce people who do not know anyone, know who needs a refill of food or drink and what is happening in other parts of the house – a child that needs attention or something happening in the kitchen. In other words, you have optimum awareness and are on top of the situation in every way and are at your natural best. You are comfortable and in command of your space.

An understanding of your personal space, and the ingredients and tools for making it work for you, will give you the ability to create a comfortable home for yourself and those around you. Fear, worry and faulty perception cause this portable home to shrink and atrophy. What follow are some ways of becoming aware of these tools and of developing a positive and meaningful presence.

OBSERVATIONS AND EXERCISES

Note: Most of the exercises in this book are designed with busy people in mind. They can be done in three minutes!

Observations

Having read this chapter, begin to observe yourself and those around you more carefully. Notice the following:

❏ Your own physical awareness of expansiveness.
❏ Are there others around you who seem to have presence?
❏ What are their qualities?
❏ At what times and in what situations are you most at home?
❏ At what times are you most comfortable? Why?
❏ What happens to the body when someone is happy, sad, at ease, uncomfortable?

❑ Do people shrink noticeably when around senior executives or others perceived to be very important?

❑ How many people in your working environment see others around them?

❑ What are the general awareness levels around you?

❑ Are you aware of the times when you are fully present? For example, when you walk through the office is your internal dialogue such that you barely notice those in your path – or at the sides?

EXERCISES

1. *180-degree vision*
   (a) Extend your arms straight out in front of you, palms touching.
   (b) While keeping your eyes straight ahead, slowly open your arms out to the side. Notice where your peripheral vision stops. Note how much you can see without moving your eyes.
   (c) While looking straight ahead, describe the detail you see in front, on the sides, upwards and downwards.
   (d) Practise this (without the arms) while walking somewhere in the office, down the street, etc.

2. *Awareness*
   You can do this when you first arrive at work.
   (a) Sit quietly with both feet flat on the floor.
   (b) Spend three minutes making a list of the following:
   Sounds you hear, temperature, air flow in the room, smells, colours, the feel of your desk, the general mood, the location of other people, are they seated or moving about?
   (c) Become aware of the area outside the room. What things do you sense from that direction?

4

VISIBILITY AND IMAGE: THE PHYSICAL AND MENTAL YOU

The physical characteristics of a confident person include a balanced, easy posture, seeing eyes and a pleasant, freely produced voice. As stated earlier, 55 per cent of personal communication is that which is visible while a person is talking. In this section, posture and alignment, which form a large part of the visible aspects, will be discussed in relation to health, image and voice.

A NOTE ABOUT CONFIDENCE

The characteristics above are the outward manifestations of confidence. All of these things are changeable and you do not need confidence to make the changes. You need only good guidance and teaching, and the willingness to improve yourself.

Confidence is an end-product. You do not have to wait for the confidence to do something. Confidence is gained as part of the process of doing it. The discussion that follows includes tools for developing confidence. Sometimes it takes courage to use those tools and to live with a change of habits. Do not confuse courage with confidence. Most of us have courage even when we think we do not have confidence.

PHYSICAL ALIGNMENT AND ITS RELATIONSHIP TO HEALTH, ENERGY, IMAGE AND VOICE

Like many of us, you have no doubt been told to stand up straight, get your shoulders back and not to slump – in many instances to no avail. Such directions seem strange and rigid and do not fit in with our self-concepts. Furthermore, it is virtually impossible to correct posture on the basis of verbal instructions. Physical alignment and posture relate to our kinaesthetic awareness of our position in time and space. We have to feel changes in alignment. Verbal directions for posture are simply not as helpful. People will do their best to follow such directions. However, since few of us know the feeling of straight, it is an exercise in futility.

CASE STUDY

In my seminars, after we have discussed good posture, I ask the group to tell a volunteer how to stand. The result is a very strange looking person. We all have a good laugh and then there is no problem understanding the physical and sensory nature of where we are in time and space.

Any time we begin to change our habits it causes havoc with the internal message systems for a short time. This is why how we feel and how we look are not the same. For example, if you have a tendency to lean to your right and someone comes along and straightens you, you will feel as if you are leaning to the left. However, on looking in the mirror, you will see that you are straight. For this reason, when making any physical alterations in posture or stance, it is wise to use a mirror. You will not be convinced until you see it for yourself. The most useful tool is the video camera, because you will see yourself more objectively.

Good posture defined

Researchers are agreed generally on the basic elements of a physical alignment that is efficient, uses gravity to an advantage and causes the least stress on the body in standing, sitting and moving. When you are properly aligned, a plumb-line can be dropped beside you that will fall through the centre of the ear, the point of the shoulder, the highest point of your hip, just behind the kneecap and just in front of the ankle. Your weight is balanced evenly between the heels and balls of the feet. When sitting, the only difference is that the knees are bent. The line from the head to the hips remains the same.

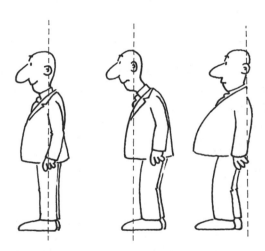

When any of these points deviate from the line, the body will have to work hard against gravity to keep you balanced. For example, when someone habitually pushes their head forward, the bottom will move out to balance it. The people who pull their chins inwards usually protrude the chest or belly to equalize the balance. Such imbalances cause your muscles to have to do an immense amount of extra work which puts an excess strain on the whole postural system.

Over time, these imbalances become bad habits, which you think feel comfortable, and you label them 'natural'. Your physical computer (brain) is now programmed to automatically use the bad habit of choice. Now when you begin to change these, you feel 'unnatural'. It is easy to confuse the word 'natural' with the word 'habitual' in such circumstances. However, it hinders our progress when we think that changing a bad habit is 'unnatural'.

The quickest way to change your posture is to be physically shown (places to seek help with physical alignment and movement: Alexander Technique, Feldenkrais Practitioners, Yoga, Pilates and good dance classes). This involves someone else moving your body until the alignment is correct and balanced. Because this new alignment is different to your old habit, it will feel strange – just like any change. Remember, you will need to see yourself to be convinced that you do not look as weird as you feel.

Your body is comprised of a dynamic, vibrating mass of atoms. Therefore posture is also dynamic rather than a static, held position. By giving each of these atoms space to vibrate, we become 'expanded humans'. This enables you to be well balanced with gravitational forces, increases the space between joints and allows flexibility and ease of movement and muscle action and eases breathing. Being static or fixed leads to rigidity and stiffness, creates discomfort and pain and makes you look uneasy.

Physical rigidity creates potential health problems, slows spontaneity and makes thinking difficult. When working on your posture, make sure you get up, move around and shake your arms and shoulders. It is easy to try to hold on to any new position or feeling. Basically we have to recreate it all the time. Staying loose is important and is not to be confused with the concept that many people have regarding being casual. Balanced alignment will allow you to look and feel lighter and taller and to move easily.

'Casual' and 'relaxed' defined

The first reaction of many people who have had their posture corrected is to think they now look formal rather than relaxed. Muscles do only two things: they contract to shorten and move a joint or they relax or let go. When muscles relax, your joints move further apart, creating more space and allowing expansion of your body. In other words, relaxing is the opposite to what many people think. The casual and relaxed posture that most people exhibit in reality is more like a collapsed heap. In my seminars, we often have to redefine the word relaxed, as used by most people, to collapsed – certainly where posture is concerned. If you could see an X-ray of your skeleton during your 'relaxed' posture, you would see vertebrae that were pushed onto each other, creating a lot of pressure on the vertebral disc and the joint itself. Over time with such pressure, the discs begin to erode or collapse and infringe on the spinal nerves. This degeneration leads to all kinds of pain.

Health and energy

Physical alignment is linked inexorably to good health. We deny this with excuses such as, 'That is just the way I am' or 'It is natural for me'. We forget the years of habits that have contributed to our current way of behaving. The folly of this response only sinks in when the body demands to be heard in the form of discomfort and pain.

When you are in a good, balanced alignment, there is space between joints for mobility, the vertebrae are balanced on each other, there is room in the chest to breathe more easily and the internal organs are easily mobile and not cramped. Any other way of being is going to create problems given enough time. The most common problems have to do with the back.

Back pain is the most common cause of days missed from work. While we can blame the chairs, long hours of sitting, etc, we are still responsible and have a choice in the way we sit. It can seem like too much effort at first. However, after sitting properly for even a week, you will begin to notice that it becomes uncomfortable to sit poorly. Your body has begun to let you know.

When your chair is too high, sit forward and put your feet flat on the floor or a footrest. There is no rule that says you have to use the backs of chairs. Your back is capable of supporting itself, it does not need to lean on a chair. When you remain dynamic, your body will cope without a backrest. However, if you try to hold yourself up or fix a particular position, you will become stiff and your muscles will complain. A good chair will help but will not solve the problem necessarily. Ultimately, it is up to you to sit properly lest your back takes the strain. Going to a good osteopath or chiropractor can help sort you out. However, they are no substitute for the work you can do on yourself.

Any joint that is not balanced will begin to show wear and tear. For example, people who have the habit of sitting with their feet twisted or the weight on the outside of the ankle will, over a period of time, begin to stretch the outside ligaments that stabilize the joint. The foot will begin to remember that pattern and on a microscopic level will begin to exhibit an uneven walking pattern. One day, that person will sprain their ankle because of a build-up of poor habits – not really an accident. When I ask for a show of hands as to who in my seminars has ankle problems, the ones sitting with the outsides of their feet on the floor raise their hands.

The same is true of any joint. The habits we have eventually distort the true natural alignment and we begin to have so-called accidents. Those people who cross their legs when sitting are pulling the pelvis out of line each time they do that. If they cross one leg the majority of the time, the pelvis and spine will be pulled in that direction. This causes the pelvis on one side to come forward and twists the spine in that direction. The muscles of the back adjust and over time there will be a scoliosis of the spine (a lateral S-shaped curve in the vertebral column); one hip will be higher and one leg slightly shorter. Now the walking pattern will change and again the body will have to work incredibly hard to keep its balance. Inattention to balance may work when we are teenagers; however, as we get older, the body will take its revenge. It is never too late to correct the problem but takes more effort after the habit is ingrained. However, you *can* teach an old dog new tricks when the old dog is willing to learn and the rewards are great enough.

Another area affected greatly by alignment is our breathing patterns. Breathing is a reflex action that occurs approximately 24 400 times a day. The efficiency of this act can be hindered enormously by the state of your posture. Our oxygen supply is very important to good health and having free unrestricted breathing is imperative. Because breath is vital to life, the body will take it in any way it can. It is our duty to make it easier by standing properly.

Adequate oxygenation of the blood is dependent on the efficiency of our breathing and contributes to our sense of well-being and energy. When you are in a sunken state of collapse, the chest is pulled down towards the abdomen and the contents of both areas are compacted. This makes it impossible for the diaphragm to do its work, the lungs do not have adequate space and breathing becomes shallower and shallower, gradually restricting the oxygen supply.

Image

People with an air of ease about them have a radiant energy and look special. While image includes clothes and other factors, they become less significant when confronted with a radiant person. This is an image built from your physical, mental and emotional ease. However, this radiance can be obscured by doing something that is outlandish or out of keeping with you as a person or the occasion. For example, if you wear jeans to a black tie affair, you will be out of balance and out of keeping with the occasion. Your actions may be interpreted to mean that you do not respect your hosts or the situation. While you may stand tall, say brilliant things and be a most interesting person, you will not be remembered for what you said or how interesting you were – only for your inappropriate dress. On the other hand, the best clothes in the world will not look good on a slumping body. Posture and physical alignment are vital to your impact.

It takes only minor physical changes to create an impression you do not intend. One of the most common postural faults is that of shortening the back of the neck and throwing the head back, thereby causing the chin to lift upwards. This creates a number of physical problems. First, with the chin up in the air, you must look down your nose in order to see. This in turn causes the eye muscles that pull the eyes into that position to become stronger. When this fault is corrected by bringing the head into alignment, people sometimes feel like they are looking at the floor. They have to be made aware that eye movements are separate from the head and can be readjusted with the new head position.

This position of chin in the air is interpreted by others to mean 'stuck up', haughty, proud, snooty, etc. Most people exhibiting this postural pattern say to me, 'People think I am being conceited when I'm not'. As soon as the head is aligned, they are no longer accused of being that way.

Body language

One of the most discussed areas associated with image is that of perceived body language. Looking at body language from a cultural perspective is fascinating. Using it as a tool for judgement and analysis creates a number of communication difficulties. How nice it would be if everyone saw and described the physical nature of a person without needing to add an interpretation. Such interpretation invites unnecessary judgement and hinders the process of communication.

When you are busy analysing someone's body language, you are somewhere in your head and not fully present. You cannot listen to another person and analyse at the same time. They will not feel comfortable talking with you. Being there for another person means no judgement. How are we to know whether the twitch in the left shoulder is a nerve problem, an injury or a strange habit? When we are occupied with trying to remember whether that twitch means the person is a thief, liar, etc or if this is a closed person because the arms are folded in front, we will never find out much about him or her. Accepting people as they are is primary to good communication skills.

A note about hair

An audience will get many clues about you from your face and expressions. Therefore it is very important that your face, and especially your eyes, be seen. While you may feel comfortable with your hair hanging around or in your face, your audience may not. Hairstyles need to be planned carefully for any public appearance.

CASE STUDY

I was once speaking on a panel with a woman who was meticulous about her presentation and information. However, she had given no thought to her looks, particularly her hair, which was very long. She had pulled it behind her ear on her left side and allowed the right side to dangle and cover part of her face. She had a tendency to lean forward when talking to the audience so those on her right never saw her face because the long hair completely covered that side. Sadly, one half of her audience never saw any part of her face and missed some vital visual elements of her communication.

It is best to keep your hair well away from your eyes and eyebrows. Even pop singers who have hair falling in their faces block an important part of the visual aspects of their communication. For women there are a number of styles that prevent them being seen adequately. One current style is to have a long fringe or bangs that extend to the eyebrows. Again it is impossible to see part of the facial expression. All we see is a hairline that takes attention away from the eyes. It is important also to be aware of the effect of eyeglass frames. Image consultants often ask people to change frames so that more of the face is seen and that there are not too many distracting extras about the face.

Men with beards and certain types of moustache can have problems as well. Hair that covers the lips or forms unusual shapes can look exaggerated from a platform or at a distance. Beards are best trimmed to the shape of the face. The outline of your lips must be clearly seen. Otherwise, from a distance, the mouth looks like a piece of moving fur with teeth and can be quite distracting and comical for an audience. The moustache that curves downwards gives the impression that the person never smiles. From a distance it looks like a magnified frown – no matter how much you smile.

Voice

A good resonant voice is directly related to your alignment. Like any instrument, the voice must be put together properly. By maintaining a good alignment, its power source, vibrating mechanism and resonator will be connected and able to function efficiently. No one would wish to play a bent cello or clarinet. However, many people walk around with bent voices and expect them to sound good. Talking on the phone particularly seems to bring out our worst postural habits. No wonder so many messages are garbled. The better you sit and stand, the clearer your voice. Chapter 5 is devoted to the further understanding of your voice and how to use it effectively. Therefore, suffice it to say that your voice cannot reach its potential without first correcting your alignment.

GUIDELINES FOR CHECKING AND CORRECTING POSTURE

❑ Posture is dynamic. The body is made of vibrating atoms. We are never meant to hold a position.

❑ Check alignment according to a dropped 'plumb line'. Ideally this line hangs from the top of the head, through the centre of the ear, the point of the shoulder, the highest point of the hip bone, just behind the knee cap and barely in front of the ankle.

❑ Make sure the feet are placed firmly on the floor with a sense that every part of the foot is touching the floor. Feel as if you have velcro on the soles of your feet.

❑ Balance your weight evenly between the heel and ball of the foot. You can test this by rising on your toes. If you have to shift your weight forward before rising, the weight is too far back.

❑ Even the smallest changes in weight distribution and spinal alignment will feel strange at first. Some muscles will be relaxing and others will be taking on new responsibilities. They may feel strange and even ache. It is very important to remember the dynamic nature of the body and allow yourself to move rather than remain stuck or try to hold a position.

❑ Posture is related directly to physical balance, energy, health, image and voice. Changing your alignment affects every one of these areas.

EXERCISES

Reminders

Wherever possible do these exercises in front of a mirror or use your video camera. Remember, change feels strange and different. For a while use how you look as a guide rather than how you feel.

There is a tendency to stiffen the knees when you are standing taller. Make sure they are very slightly bent because when you brace your knees, your bottom tends to protrude.

Think of your joints as having very thick grease between each one – so thick that they cannot freeze into position but have to stay balanced and poised in relation to one another.

1. Standing taller

While facing a mirror, place the palm of your hand just above the crown (towards the back) of your head. Stretch the crown up to touch your hand. You will feel quite tall when you do this correctly. The back of your neck will be stretched and feel long. If you mistakenly place your hand at the very top and centre of your head and stretch, your chin will rise. This is not what you want. Just placing a hand over the crown will remind most people to stand taller. You can do this at any time when you are standing or sitting.

As a reminder to stand tall, place Post-it notes on your mirrors, your desk, especially by your phone, on top of presentation notes or anywhere that your eyes will fall during the course of your day. This way you will not have to think of what you need to do, the reminders will do it for you. A week of doing this will begin to programme your postural muscles to perform a different set of habits.

2. Finding your balance

You are centred when your weight is evenly balanced between the balls of your feet and your heels. Many people have their weight much too far back. You can test this by rising on your toes. If you first have to rock forward before you can rise, your weight is too far back. This would be very obvious if you were able to look at yourself sideways on.

To alter your balance, first plant your feet firmly as if you had Velcro on the bottom of your shoes. Become aware of the sensitivity of your feet and allow the whole foot to feel the floor (even with shoes on). Gently rock forward from the ankle joint until the weight is evenly distributed between the balls of your feet and your heels. Any adjustment other than at the ankles will alter your spine and cause you to lose your stretch.

3. Giving every atom space

Think of each of your atoms as needing its own private space. Allow your body to expand and stretch in all directions to accommodate this vision. As you walk from place to place, feel you are getting taller with each step. Imagine that at the end of the day you will be taller than you were in the morning. Aim to be 10 feet tall and 6 feet wide by the end of the day.

4. Feeling of stretch for breathing

Lie on the floor on your back, hands by your sides. Slowly stretch your fingers as far away from your shoulders as possible without allowing your arms to leave the floor. Now breathe in while mentally counting to eight, slide your arms along the floor until they are overhead. Breathe out to an eight count and slide your arms back to the starting position. This exercise will help you keep your chest expanded and encourage movement of your abdomen during breathing.

5

IMPROVE YOUR VOICE

Even the most beautiful of people can be betrayed by an unpleasant or unsuitable voice. This was particularly evident when movies changed from silent to sound. Suddenly the most ravishing men and women became laughing stocks because no attention had been paid to their voices. The vocal 38 per cent of communication took on massive importance.

In some ways, the voice is the most deeply personal aspect of communication. Physically, it lives inside of us and seems untouchable. Because the voice comes from the inside, we are fooled into thinking that we have no control of it. The sound is affected by emotions and tensions, mental and physical. For this reason the voice is considered to be the most difficult aspect of ourselves to change. This misconception is due mainly to faulty perceptions about our own sound and ignorance about how the voice works. Once you understand, you can choose whether you wish to make any changes or not. Change in this case means creating more variety in pitch, expression, tone colour, rhythm — all the things you do easily when you are comfortable, feeling at home and not being self-conscious.

HOW THE VOICE WORKS: AN OVERVIEW

Your voice is like any other musical instrument in that it has a power supply, breath; a vibrator, the larynx; and a resonator, the throat or pharynx. The housing for this instrument is your body.

Therefore the alignment of your body is the first step to connecting the parts of your instrument. The efficiency, quality and depth of your sound depend on this connection.

Sound is made by air moving up through the larynx, causing the vocal cords (most accurately described as folds) to vibrate. These vibrations are then magnified and modified in the spaces of the throat, mouth and nose, in the case of nasalized sounds. Actions of the lips, tongue, palate and jaw provide the vowels and consonants of speech. Any distortion in the movement of these structures will have a direct effect on the quality of the voice.

Power source

There is no sound without air to carry it. Your voice needs a steady, supported stream of air to function at its best. The more efficient your breathing patterns, the more effective will be your voice – and health. During a normal day we breathe approximately 24 400 times. Breath is responsible for maintaining the acid-base balance in the body and regulated by a subconscious body reflex system.

Air is crucial to life, so the body will use any means necessary to breathe. However, basic to good voice use is an efficient system of air intake and release. Efficient, easy breathing is dependent upon physical alignment, lack of tension in the neck, throat and mouth and the actual physical patterns we use to allow air in and out.

Most people become concerned about how they take air in. I suggest that you concern yourself with how you expel air first. This will allow the in-breath to become a reflex action and the support mechanism to function naturally. When we cry, cough, wail, groan or sob or use what are sometimes referred to as primal sounds, the muscles of the abdomen and back of the waist engage. You can feel this when you put one hand on the lowest part of your abdomen (well below your belt) and one hand on your waistband towards the back and use any of the above sounds. You can also feel this abdominal pressure when you use the sounds 'pshhhhh' forcefully or rolled r's – as if you are revving up an engine. At the end of this expulsion of air and sound, the abdomen will release to allow more air to enter. All this is done without any interference from the throat, lips and tongue.

As you make these sounds you are using a strong abdominal muscle action to support the sound. Ideally, this is what you will do in speaking as well. This action does not have to be forceful or punched; the abdominal muscles need to be engaged. This will give you a sense of being connected to your whole body and prevent you from substituting tensions in the chest or head and neck area. The ensuing sounds will have substance and there will be minimal wear and tear on your throat and larynx.

Vibrator or sound source

Your larynx or structure, of which your Adam's apple is a part, houses the vocal folds. The vocal folds are like two shelves made up of muscles, a small piece of cartilage and other elastic membranes and ligaments. They are located in the larynx, which sits at the top of the windpipe (trachea). These folds first act as a protector of your lungs by keeping out foreign matter, and secondly as your source of vocal sound.

You have probably had some experience with the protective aspect. Normally when you swallow, the vocal folds close tightly to prevent food from entering the lungs. However, if you have ever tried to talk and eat at the same time, you may have had the unpleasant experience of something going 'down the wrong way'. The resulting gagging is the protective action of the vocal folds at work. They are so sensitive that it takes something smaller than three microns in diameter to get through them.

When you wish to make sound, air comes from the lungs through the vocal folds. They close – or move closer together – and begin to vibrate. You can get an idea of how this works by blowing up a balloon and then stretching the mouth of it. The squeal that follows is distantly related to the way the vocal folds make sound.

The regulation of pitch and the heaviness or lightness of voice involve the action of the vocal folds. The pitch will rise when the folds are elongated and the voice becomes heavy when they are thickened.

Any tension in the neck around the larynx will inhibit the vibratory pattern of the folds. You may recognize this as some of the strangled sounds you and others produce when you are afraid. You know the situation – high chest breathing, neck tension, larynx high under your jaw – self-strangulation. Untrained speakers and singers often try to do it this way. It is important to maintain the emphasis in the abdominal area so that the chest and laryngeal areas can function easily and naturally with no effort.

The co-ordination of breath and vocal fold closure is important for the onset of the sound. When there is inadequate closure the sound is breathy. Usually this is caused by a combination of poor posture, faulty breathing and a lack of energy. If the vocal folds are tightly closed, as in holding your breath, the beginning of the sound can become harsh and strident. This is caused by pressurized air held below the folds being emitted forcibly as you begin a word. Many people speak as if they are trying to hold on or save their air. This may come from old ideas of not having enough air or attempting to control the breath from the chest or neck. Such habits are abusive and over time can cause the voice to become hoarse or create more serious vocal disturbances.

The resonator

Aesthetically, the most important area of the voice is resonance. The quality of the voice is unique with every individual and is difficult to quantify. Voice quality is determined by the shape of the throat (pharynx), general vocal and whole body co-ordination and imagination. Very few people reach their potential and optimum quality when it comes to how they use their voices.

Anatomically, the resonating area of the voice is extremely complex. It is a soft, muscular, sleeve-like structure that is capable of assuming an infinite variety of shapes and formations. There are intimate connections with the jaw, tongue, lips and larynx. Any distortion of movement in these areas strongly affects the movement and shapes of the vocal tract and resonating chambers. The muscular actions that give us our individual qualities come from the habits and patterns we develop, family background and local and regional environments. Each of us will have slightly different and unique patterns.

Not only do various muscular patterns alter the quality of sound but the emotions play a very large role as well. You probably have noticed when a friend is feeling well or unwell just by the sound of the voice. Emotions can cause subconscious changes in the way you make sound and alter the quality.

Because the pharynx is a dual pathway for food and air, we sometimes speak by constricting these muscles as we do during swallowing. For food to move into the oesophagus, muscles at the back of the throat have to contract to squeeze it downwards. This constricts the throat and raises the larynx – the opposite of what we need for a good voice. A number of people unwittingly speak in the swallowing position and produce tense, garbled sounds. For optimum voice quality and depth of sound, the throat/pharynx must be wide and released with a continuous free flow of air.

Articulation

The formation of words is done by the articulators – the lips, tongue, teeth and hard and soft palate and the jaw. These structures help shape the resonator in such a way as to create the vowels and consonants needed for words. The vowels are shaped in the throat and mouth by various positions of the tongue, soft palate and lips. Consonants are formed by the action of the tongue, palate, lips, teeth and minimally the jaw.

Relaxed tongue and lips work far more efficiently and produce clear speech. Some people speak comfortably and easily on a one-to-one-basis. However, to ensure clarity when in front of a group, they exaggerate their articulation by distorting the movement of the lips and tongue. This is unnecessary and often is unsightly, abnormal-looking and affects the quality of the sound.

Efficient articulation for speech will involve minimal movement of the jaw. Ideally, it will be suspended, flexible and free to respond to the need of the moment. Any undue tightness such as clenching of the teeth, jamming the jaw downwards or protrusion will affect the shape of the pharynx and soft palate, the movements of the tongue and indirectly the larynx.

The speech patterns we develop derive from our parents, friends, local and national cultural practices initially, with additional patterns adopted for reasons of psychological and physical balance. These become a set of predominant muscular habits that shape the way vowels and consonants are made by each individual. This is sometimes called 'accent' or regional dialect. There is nothing wrong with an accent as long as it is clear and free. When efficient habits of speech are balanced with good physical alignment, the articulation becomes easier and clearer. What appear to be heavy, regional accents become understandable and much less distorted. Sometimes this is all that is needed to understand a previously garbled voice.

PHYSICAL HABITS THAT INTERFERE WITH VOICE AND MESSAGE

Voice quality, your message and its underlying meaning are linked to facial expression and the physical habits you exhibit both consciously and unconsciously. What follows is a rogue's gallery of common habits that can lead to questions, doubts or misinterpretation on the part of your audience.

1. *Furrowed brows or wrinkled foreheads.* Many people who are very serious tend to show this with excess tension around and above the eyes. Presenters with these habits can sound very intense when saying something very light or casual. When they do this the face and voice become hard and contradict the intended message.

2. *Tense lips.* This habit tends to make the speaker sound terse and have a rather reedy, white sound. The sound usually lacks warmth. Saying 'I love you' with tense lips can look and sound funny.

3. *Constant or fixed smile.* This has the opposite effect of number one above. Someone with a fixed smile will never convince the other person of being serious or can be taken for a person who is not being truthful. Church choir sopranos have been known to look like this. The resulting voice quality is shallow and lacking in resonance.

4. *The deadpan face.* Someone who perceives control to be maintaining an expressionless face will find that everything else about him will be dull as well. It is very difficult to get anything other than a monotone voice from a person with this habit.

5. *The tense tongue.* It is common for speakers trying to make a bigger sound to create tension in the throat and especially in the tongue. The resulting sound can be guttural or garbled and the articulation muddy.

6. *The anatomical neck.* People who are exceedingly tense and use a lot of pressure to speak will often display clear outlines of the muscles and structure of the neck. This can be seen in many rock and pop singers. Sound under this kind of pressure is unpleasant to hear.

7. *The 'determined' jaw.* A strong, overly firm or held jaw distorts voice quality immensely. It will give a person a look and sound of defiance.

In my seminars I have a crazy exercise in which I ask people to choose one sentence or phrase to be used throughout. They and their partners say this sentence using each of the habits outlined above. They are asked to make a note of how each example sounds and looks and of their gut-reaction to each habit demonstrated by their partners. There is always a great deal of laughter because some of the sentences seem so ridiculous done that way. However, there is also a general recognition that they all know someone who looks and sounds exactly like the exercises.

Stand in front of a mirror and try this for yourself. If nothing else, you will have a good laugh. Tape record this session and you will find many changes in voice quality as your expression is altered. If you have any of these mannerisms or habits, speak or read in front of a mirror so you can change what you are doing. When you want to stop a habit, you can.

Summary

Your voice will work best when you are connected by an aligned, balanced body that powers and supports the voice with use of the muscles of the abdomen and back of the waist. This connection encourages the air to flow freely through vocal folds that are unimpeded by neck or chest tension. Absence of tension in the neck and jaw create a throat that is flexible and responsive. The shape of the throat and resonating areas will respond to the emotion, imagination and intention of the speaker (or singer) and the articulation of words will be audible and clear.

The physically free and efficient functioning of the voice sets up the possibility for a beautiful, natural sound that is a true representation of you. Your connection to this sound enables you to let your imagination, intuition and creativity trigger spontaneous interaction with the messages you are conveying. You are then ready to fill your personal space with sound – as if your voice is coming from every pore in your body (360-degree sound). There is no need to think of pointing or projecting your voice. Simply fill your space, which can be expanded to include as many people as you like.

CASE STUDY

A woman in a very senior position consulted me because she was told she could not be heard at meetings. This lady was powerful in her role and in her person. I was shocked to learn that her voice was letting her down. During a consultation in her office I was seated directly across from her. There was nothing obviously wrong with her voice or her posture and her speech was clear. As we talked, I noticed that she seemed very withheld. So I asked her what would happen if I leaned forward into her space. Without hesitation she said she would move away from me immediately. I then asked her how far she felt her personal space extended. Her space was defined as being about one to two feet in front of her. She believed she needed to protect herself and felt extremely vulnerable in extending her space further. After some discussion and experimentation, she began to think of her space as much larger. When she did, her voice began to fill it. She realized that she had been talking to her own protective wall. As the wall fell away, her voice began to fill the space. She no longer has a problem being heard at meetings.

BEING EXPRESSIVE

Words and language developed as a way of describing pictures and feelings. Words have an inherent meaning and expressive people convey it when they speak. Too often presenters go through the words without any consideration of the voice or expression – as if the information and words themselves were enough. Your voice reflects the extent of your energy, feelings, enthusiasm and imagination. The energy comes from both the physical connection of your voice and your passion for your topic, the feelings from your perceptions, background and sensitivity regarding the subject and your imagination will furnish the colour and sparkle or the twinkle in your eyes.

This is another area where our perception of what we are doing and the actual sound that is being produced is extremely misleading. In order to become better, many people have to go over-the-top by a huge amount just to look and sound normal or plausible. My clients only believe this when they have seen it for themselves on the video playback. Were they not to have this facility, 99 per cent of them would simply not believe what was being told them by anyone. When they see it for themselves, there is instantaneous recognition of the need to change and self-permission to do more than they thought was ever needed.

Going over-the-top means taking what seems like a huge risk. This is one of those areas where courage is necessary. It is easier to do when the task involves something whimsical or imaginative. I use children's stories in my seminars. Often we get so involved that we are dissatisfied when there is not enough time to finish each story.

Children's stories

Any time you think you are exaggerating, it is best to use a video for feedback. Otherwise you will never go far enough because you will be convinced in your own mind that you have done it already. Here is a way to work on your expressiveness. Choose material such as a children's story or fable to read aloud. This exercise demands spontaneity. The more you think about it, the more difficult it is. Allow yourself to become completely involved in the story. If you feel embarrassed to do this exercise, close the door and ham it up in front of your mirror. Give yourself permission to be a fool or a clown momentarily. Read this three times – each time a little differently and record yourself on video or tape recorder:

EXERCISES

1.   Read two or three minutes of the text in the way you might read to children.
2.   Read another two or three minutes of text making sure that you have given each of the characters an appropriate voice, ie, a bear or lion voice, or a little girl or boy voice, etc. When no characters have dialogue, choose important or colourful words to emphasize.
3.   The third time read and act out the text at the same time. Pretend half of your audience is deaf and you must show them the story. This means that if the text reads, 'They walked down a very long road', you will demonstrate this with your hand at the same time by 'walking' with your fingers down a long road. You

will probably feel much like a ham actor. However, persist, because it is important. While you are busy carrying out this ridiculous exercise, your voice will be gaining colour, giving each word its true meaning, your pace will fit the text rather than having the same pitch and rhythm throughout.

4. Now find several paragraphs of a company report, news article, advert, a business letter you have written or received, and read this in the same way as you did the final version of the children's story. Be careful because this is where your preconceptions of how you 'ought' to be in a business setting will get in the way. Believe it or not, the words can be just as colourful. It is possible to demonstrate words like dichotomy, bottom line, procedure, large undertaking, etc. Make sure that named people are shown to be in different places so that they will sound like different people. John Smith and Jo Martin are different and need to sound like it. People and grocery lists can sound the same when there is no vision of what the words mean in the mind of the speaker.

This exercise builds in the very things needed most in our conversation and presentation. By acting out the story or the company report, you develop a spontaneous rhythm and sensibility to the words, the pace is appropriate, pauses come naturally rather than being contrived, the pitch and colour of the voice respond to your imagination and mental pictures. It stops the measured monosyllabic approach to what are perceived as formal presentations.

My clients have found this exercise to be of great benefit in changing their perceptions about their presentations. What they thought was over-the-top looked like a normal expressive human being to them. What they perceived to be expressive was dull, bland and basically – boring.

CASE STUDY

Sometimes when a client comes to me for voice work, I find that it is not really the voice itself that needs correcting but some other area that is affecting the voice.

Rob came to me because he was being interviewed for an important executive job and wanted to stand the best chance of getting it. When I asked him what he thought would hold him back, he shared the information that others felt he lacked 'gravitas'. His voice tended to be a bit high pitched and did not sound fully connected with his body, so he was robbed of some of his resonance. I noticed as he sat he was constantly moving his feet and that they were never on the floor. I asked him to place both feet on the floor and keep them still. Suddenly his voice was deeper, he sounded far more serious and he began to sound like an executive. Just keeping the feet on the floor quietened his body enough for his voice to connect. We worked on other areas of his presentation but the voice was by far the most dramatic change. He got the job.

SUMMARY: WORKING WITH YOUR VOICE

❑ You can improve almost any voice by balancing the physical alignment of the body. It is particularly important to make sure the head is positioned over the shoulders rather than poked forward or tilting backwards. When a person is connected physically and well-grounded with feet firmly on the floor, the voice is much more resonant and pleasant.

❑ Power and efficient use of breath come from supporting the sound from the lower abdominal area. We do this naturally when we laugh, cough, cry or moan. Using any of these sounds can help you get a feel for what 'support' means. Any physical tensions around the shoulder and neck will disengage the abdominal support and constrict the area around the larynx and throat.

❑ It is best to treat the in-breath as a reflex of the out-breath. Breathe out using a 'psst' or a 'hiss' until you are completely out of air. The reflex in-take of air will usually be correct and cause the lower abdominal area to expand. At the on-set of sound this area is then contracted to provide support.

❑ Airflow is essential for quality of sound. 'Saving' air creates tension at the level of the larynx and inhibits the sound.

❏ Optimal voice quality comes from good alignment and free neck and throat areas. Any tensions around the neck, mouth and jaw will cause a change in voice quality and a more strangled sound. Physical habits that indicate tension include: furrowed brows, glaring eyes, a deadpan face, tight lips, an exaggerated smile, any deviation of the jaw from a central position, a held jaw or clenched teeth, an overly opened mouth, raised shoulders and clavicular breathing.

❏ Colour in the voice comes from free, uninhibited imagination while speaking (or singing) and presenting. This is enabled by the ability to picture everything that is being said. Every word has onomatopoetic qualities and we tend to forget this in business. Use of hands to help make the picture will often free the voice and allow much more expression.

❏ Use of singing or singsong can help voices that are hesitant or brittle. A continuous sound has a kind of resonant hum that is always present. Singing a text will help the airflow as well as continuity of sound and phrasing.

EXERCISES TO IMPROVE VOICE AND EXPRESSION

1. Breathing and support

   (a) To get a feeling for breathing without shoulder movement or chest tension, do the following: sit on a chair or stool, feet flat on the floor, and let your body fold over so that your chest is resting fully on your thighs, your arms and head hanging down loosely. Take in a big breath. Without chest and shoulder involvement on the in-breath, you will feel the action of your abdomen expanding against your thighs and your back expanding behind. This is the area that needs to be active when you are standing.

   (b) While standing (or sitting in a chair) do the following: first check your alignment and make sure that your head is over your shoulders. Then stretch your arms over your head, without raising your shoulders, clasp your fingers and turn your palms towards the sky. While maintaining this stretch, using a hissing sound or the 'pshhh', let air out until you feel you have released your last drop. The reflex in-breath is likely to be felt and seen in the expansion of the abdominal wall and back.

(c) Visualize an open pipe extending from your mouth to a place just above your pubic bone. Think of your breath as travelling both to and from that area without restriction anywhere in the pipeline.

(d) Place Post-it notes at your desk, on your telephone and in your car to remind you to breathe from a deep place.

(e) When sitting, support your voice by feeling your tummy button moving towards the back of your chair as you speak.

2. *Releasing tension and freeing the neck*

When we become stressed, one of the first places to show it is the voice. There is a tendency for the breath to be high and for the throat to become a 'bottleneck'. The voice can become strident and harsh – not what we want when doing our best to communicate well.

(a) Release any tendency to hold in the neck area by gently and slowly moving your head from side to side while breathing and speaking (as if maintaining a continual 'no–no' motion of your head). Make sure you do not stop the movement to take in air or to begin a sentence. Think of your head as being poised on top of a heavily greased joint. Most people tend to stop this motion to speak or breathe and cause momentary blockage of the speech mechanism. Watch yourself in a mirror to make sure you are not doing this. Either read or talk aloud to do this exercise.

(b) Use more air than you think you need. Your vocal folds will not vibrate easily without adequate air. Read a passage from a book or newspaper with an extremely breathy voice. Remember, what it sounds like in your head is not the same as it does to others.

3. Increasing depth and resonance

When you have done the previous exercises and gained more vocal freedom, you will find that already your voice is showing increased depth and resonance. The more centred you are, the more quality you will have in your sound. Imagine your voice as being at one with all the millions of atoms that vibrate in your body. This will give you and your voice a sense of depth without effort and will also fill the space around you.

4. Articulation

Efficient and flexible use of your tongue, lips and jaw is the key to clear articulation. Again, if you have paid attention to the previous exercises, your articulation will be better without additional effort. Any exaggerated movements of the structures above will distort your diction. Commonly, when someone is asked to speak more clearly and distinctly, the response is to begin to exaggerate movements of the lips and jaw. This creates a comical look and strange sounds. A released jaw, no exaggerated movement and flexible tongue and lips are the key to efficient articulation.

Any book on diction will give you exercises for every vowel and consonant. This is not the purpose of this book. However, be aware of several potential problem areas:

(a) Look in a mirror to see that your tongue tip is in the front of your mouth when you pronounce S's, Z's and R's. When the tongue deviates to one side, the diction is distorted and may sound like a speech impediment.

(b) Check to see that the consonants made by the lips, like F's, V's, B's and M's, are made directly in front as well. It is a common habit in some cultures to distort these sounds.

5. Expression

Practise going over-the-top about everything you say – in private, of course. This kind of practice will plant seeds that you will use in your communication and presentations. Your natural reticence will stop you from going too far. So rest assured that you will use about 10 per cent of what you have practised. Gradually, as you become braver, you will get a feel for a good balance.

6

Listening and rapport

LISTENING

When in doubt, listen. It is one of the best ways to establish rapport. Being a good listener takes patience and is a skill rarely taught. In the haste to 'get to the bottom line' or to appear that we know it already or to be perceived as precocious, we rush in with comments and questions, hardly waiting for the end of the sentence, much less the thought. When we are mentally impatient, we interrupt without hearing the other person finish his or her 'paragraph'. Our busy minds are like radios, chattering away, analysing, comparing and hearing very little. By remaining mentally quiet, silent and listening long enough, most of our questions will be answered.

Leave the internal analysis and questions for later. Listening with an open, accepting mind creates an atmosphere of trust in which discussions and issues can be pursued in a rational and logical manner. Communicators who know how to do this create a situation in which others can be themselves.

The analogy of the computer is useful here. When listening, think of yourself as a blank computer screen. You have information and knowledge stored on your hard disk – the brain. To put new information in your computer you need a clean screen. There is no need to edit or analyse or judge the information as you write it down. This can be done later after you have had time to decide what is appropriate to store.

Trust your mind and knowledge. It is not going to go away for the short time you are listening to someone else. To attempt to listen at the same time as internally repeating or memorizing your question or statement is another form of internal sabotage. It is a great temptation to hold on to our own knowledge while at the same time trying to understand the information we are receiving.

Neither of you will communicate unless one of you hears the other person fully. It is important to accept that the other person is speaking his or her truth at that moment. Whether you agree or disagree is not the issue. By remaining quiet inside, you will be able to sort out the issue in a rational manner. This will allow the speaker the freedom to change his mind or alter his stance without losing face. You are then in a better position to respond from the vantage points of knowledge, logic, experience and wisdom.

A good way to ensure that you are listening is to offer a brief literal summary of what you have heard rather than making assumptions, which have to do with your perceptions, not necessarily the other person's statements. By summarizing you can check the accuracy of your understanding. At the same time this gives the other person a chance to hear what they have said fed back to them and allows the possibility of changing anything that is not accurate.

If, instead, you make an assumption, it can create the need for the other person to justify what they have said before they have finished a line of thought. Rather than using language such as, 'I assume you mean/or want to do...?', say, 'Tell me what you mean by that', 'Will you tell me more about...?', or, 'What would you like to do about it?'

Rather than directing conversations to yourself by saying, 'I assume/presume, etc?', focus on getting information from the other person. Ask open questions like, 'What excites you most about this project?', 'What proved to be the most difficult problem in reaching this goal?', or, 'Tell me what you need from me.' These kinds of question can be followed by asking for more detailed and specific information.

Such open questions are useful in social situations as well. For example, when you know someone likes cars, ask, 'If you could have any car you wanted, what would it be?' 'What in particular

do you like about that car?' You could substitute many different words for car – dress, kitchen, dog, house, etc. Find out what interests others and help them enjoy it. Soon enough they will ask you about yourself.

SUMMARY: THE CHARACTERISTICS OF SKILLED LISTENERS

❑ They are fully present and 'want to be here'.
❑ They listen with a quiet mind and body. (Remember that the words 'listen' and 'silent' are anagrams.)
❑ Judgement and analysis are momentarily suspended.
❑ The momentary truth of the other person is fully accepted.
❑ They summarize what they have heard and ask appropriate questions.
❑ They understand that their personal presence is their home and act as good hosts and hostesses.

ESTABLISHING RAPPORT

Wanting to be there, listening and genuine interest in the other person are ways to instant rapport. When we are fully there we will respond easily and comfortably to those around us. When you feel comfortable talking with someone, probably the rapport is established without your being conscious of it. However, it is helpful to have some fall-back mechanisms when we feel ill at ease. 'When in Rome, do as the Romans do' is worth remembering. Learning the non-verbal tools for building rapport can be extremely helpful in cultures other than your own.

The tools of rapport have been developed over a number of years from the research and study of the characteristics of good communicators (see Laborde, 1987). This is true particularly in situations where we are self-conscious – such as meeting someone for the first time, dealing with awkward situations, needing to talk with other members of staff who hold different positions, or any other time when we may not be feeling well and are nervous for some reason.

People who are communicating easily tend to look (have the same body positions) and sound alike. They exhibit similar energies. This is true whether they are happy, sad, excited or angry. You can observe this for yourself by becoming a people-watcher. Children are particularly interesting to watch. Those engaged in the same activity will look like a school of fish all moving in the same direction, then changing and all moving in another direction, looking like clones. Partners dining together will have the same physical pose and the movements of their bodies will move towards and away from each other in rhythm. Look around at a committee meeting. All those truly involved will look alike, either all sitting back or all sitting forward. When there is one who is completely different, you might question whether that person is 'there'. In fact, it would offer you an opportunity to ask that person what he thinks. That way, he would be pulled back into the group and its activities.

CASE STUDY

I once had a group of sceptics who did not believe this when we were discussing it in a seminar. However, that evening at a birthday dinner I looked up to see that there were two people at either end of the table quietly talking to those close by. At each end of the table were groups that looked exactly alike, the same posture, positions of the arms legs, etc. I asked them to freeze and then look. They were astounded.

Creating rapport is about momentarily putting yourself in the other person's shoes. It is easy to draw attention to yourself without thinking. For example, if your best friend comes in excited because she has just won the lottery, she will most likely have an animated face, voice and body, high breathing and an energetic high-pitched voice. The ideal response to that is for you to say, 'That's wonderful' and react with the same energy in body, voice and feeling. The worst response would be to fold your arms in disgust and say, 'I never win anything'. First share her joy. If you need to be disgusted, do it at home later.

CASE STUDY

In one seminar I had a woman who told me that when she saw herself looking like the person to whom she was speaking, she immediately changed. She deliberately created a mismatch of energies. According to other staff, she was unpopular and difficult to engage in team activity. No wonder! All her life, her perception was that she was supposed to be different. She had no idea that her lack of rapport was making communication difficult for her and those around her.

When rapport is discussed with those on my seminars, their first response is to think that learning about it constitutes a form of manipulation. It is not a manipulative tool – simply a way to become more observant and relate better when you are uncomfortable. Imitating someone by copying all their gestures and movements is not a responsible way to establish rapport. If you speak to someone who is copying and mimicking all of your movements and gestures, you have permission to do something outlandish. If they still copy you, find someone else to talk to. Rapport is established when you momentarily put yourself in that person's shoes. It is about matching energy.

Do not confuse energy with emotion. You can take on a similar energy without becoming involved in the emotion. You do not have to become angry when the other person is irate. You can match the tone, pitch and energy of their voice and posture and use your words and logic. For example, when someone comes in angry and hot under the collar, the worst scenario is the one in which you go into ultra slow, measured mode and ask them to calm down. This is a mismatch. You are far better off using their energy, rate of speech and pitch to say something like, 'Let's sit down and talk about it'. When you have an excitable person talking to a slow and deliberate person, one of them is going to become impatient or annoyed. Take the responsibility to match the other person. It will not be long before they begin to warm to your pace.

There are many ways to create 'common ground' or rapport – some obvious and others very subtle. Because it is natural to be in rapport, people generally do not go around looking to see who is in rapport with them. Therefore you do not need to worry about using these techniques. You can choose to match posture, breathing patterns, voice, physical rhythms – but not the same way. That constitutes mimicry, and words.

Matching posture and rhythm

The easiest way to gain rapport is to adopt the same body posture. For example, if the person's right leg is crossed, you might cross yours. You mirror their position.

Note: This means body position, *not* exact imitation of movement habits such as twiddling the fingers or various twitches of feet and hands, etc. Because I worked on my posture so much, I never altered it when I was with other people. It was much later, when I had learned about rapport, that I found out that these people perceived me as being hard to reach. I was mismatching them because I was busy being an example of good posture. My misperception was a hindrance to my communication with those around me.

Another easy way to establish rapport is to pick up their rhythms or twitches very subtly *in some other way*. For example, when someone taps his or her fingers, you gently tap your toe to his or her rhythm in a manner which is *not observable*.

Breath

Breathing in the same rhythm is subtle and very effective. (However, *not* if a person has just run the four-minute mile!) Many therapists and healers breathe with their clients as a way of establishing contact. To observe the breathing pattern, look at the area between the shoulders and neck or the chest (make sure it is with 180-degree vision or they will think you are staring).

Voice

When we share someone's happiness or sadness we usually match their tone of voice without thinking about it. Sometimes we have to do this more consciously and deliberately match the tone, energy and pitch of the other person's voice. It is not easy to do when you are in a hurry to get on with it. However, it is especially useful on the telephone where you cannot see the other person.

Words

Use similar words and phrases to the people with whom you are speaking. Be aware of words peculiar to their vocabulary and use them in your own way where it is appropriate. In other words, speak their language whenever possible.

As stated earlier, it is easy to direct conversation back to yourself unwittingly. When someone tells us about their situation we often interrupt to tell them about ours before they have had a chance to fully explain or complete a story. Yes, we all have friends or colleagues who go on and on without breathing.

However, when they eventually take a breath, you can interrupt if necessary. Sympathize when it is needed, agree when it is reasonable. These are things you usually do with friends. In general, support the person as a fellow human being.

Unconscious eye movements give us clues for verbal preferences. The brain stores information in pictures, sounds and feelings. Eye movements give clues to which system is being used. While each of us uses all of these systems, one tends to predominate. In general, the majority of the population stores information in pictures. These people will use words and phrases like, 'Let me put you in the picture', 'How do you see this?', 'I see'. This vocabulary will be a cue for you to use it because it is that person's preferred way of accessing and storing information. They will respond best when you address them in that mode. To ask people who are primarily visual how they feel about something is likely to illicit a blank stare or eyes that move in a number of directions as if searching their computers.

How do we tell which is the predominant method of accessing for each person? This takes careful observation. When you ask someone a question, watch the eyes. When they go up, right or left, or straight ahead, they are searching for a picture; eyes moving left or right on a horizontal axis signal sound or 'auditory' mode; eyes down to the right, except in some left-handed people, mean 'kinaesthetic' (feeling); eyes down to the left, except in some left-handed people, mean they are searching through verbal material for an appropriate answer or 'internal dialogue'.

A predominantly auditory person will use vocabulary such as, 'I hear you', 'How does this sound to you?', 'Does this ring any bells?' The kinaesthetic person will use words relating to sensing and feeling. All these people will respond best to vocabulary relating to their own storage systems. You can tell when you have confused them because their eyes will go through all the systems searching for an answer. That is a clue for you to rephrase or change the wording of your question or statement. It does not signify the other person's stupidity. The way we phrase questions is an important art and skill.

Values

Appreciating and listening for what a person values will furnish you with important options in presenting information, ideas or products. It is never a waste of time to explore what is dear to someone. Useful phrases for finding out what a person values include:

❏ 'What characteristics would you like to see in … a director, manager, secretary, neighbour?'
❏ 'Tell me what you like best in this type of service, product, etc?'
❏ 'If you could have anything you wanted for your organization, meeting, presentation, etc, what would it be?'
❏ Tell me what you would like instead.' (Use in response to a negative statement.)

EXERCISES RELATING TO LISTENING AND RAPPORT

1. *Listening*
   (a) Practise listening by asking a friend or colleague if you may summarize what they have said. Request feedback on the accuracy of your summary.
   (b) Listen to a whole conversation without interrupting. Note whether any questions you had were answered in the course of the conversation.
   (c) Engage in a conversation where you do not use the word 'I'. Redirect the questions to what the other person has said without stating your opinion or experience but instead asking for his or hers.
2. *Rapport*
   (a) Practise matching the following separately (you may choose a different one per day or week):
      (i) posture and alignment;
      (ii) voice;
      (iii) vocabulary.

(b) Become observant of the other person's eyes when you ask a question or during pauses when they are talking to you. Look for predominant tendencies of eye movements.

(c) Experiment with using vocabulary relating to visual, auditory or kinaesthetic characteristics. Observe the response you get. If you notice that a person looks up to find the answer, deliberately use an auditory or kinaesthetic word and note the reaction.

(d) Whenever you ask a question, note the eyes of the other person (with 180-degree vision). Never stare at another person's eyes.

(e) Experiment with asking others questions that ask for ideal solutions or positive responses. Pursue that line of questioning until you get specific positive answers that are possible.

(f) Enjoy finding out about other people and what they think. It will change the way you communicate and relate to them.

7

DEALING WITH 'FEEDBACK' AND CRITICISM

One of the most important tools for developing confidence and personal power is your ability to deal with criticism or 'feedback', the positive description of criticism. Most of us deal with it by putting up some kind of verbal or mental defence where we try to justify what we have done to cause the criticism. This behaviour causes us to turn off our listening ability, start an internal conversation and begin a process of justification and/or blame. The issue becomes personal rather than one related to the job or project.

If you want to see someone shrink, criticize them. I have seen students do this even in a role-play. The way we criticize and the way we use words is powerful, especially when they are directed negatively towards people. However, there are many in this world who do not know that, and they think that criticism is the best way to teach. There is a long history of criticism in our society that has instilled an ability for us to criticize ourselves excessively and to extend it to those around us. How we deal with inner criticism, the self-critic, has a direct bearing on how we treat others. It might be useful for you to reread Chapter 2 at this point.

ACCEPTING CRITICISM AND SUGGESTIONS

Not everyone knows how to criticize impartially and likely it will be directed to the person rather than towards the project or behaviour. It is easy to take it as a personal affront, feel offended and shrink or fight/argue.

Upon hearing criticism, your first duty is to listen and hear out the other person fully. They need to know they have been heard. Once they have been heard, you may then ask questions or for clarification. Accept that this is their truth for the moment. Accuracy, as you perceive it, is not important at this stage. First, you must acknowledge that there is a problem. The fact that the other person perceives a problem needs to be accepted by you.

Acknowledging that there is a problem does not in any way indicate that you accept blame. The focus is centred squarely on the issue, not the people involved. Play the role of detective and find out the exact nature of the problem and how the other person sees the resolution. Request specific details and ask for suggestions. Honour this person as a fellow human being whether you like him or her or not.

By the time you have done all this, the atmosphere will have changed considerably and you will have a lot of information. When you choose to argue and not hear, it is likely that both of you will go away with the issue unresolved and feeling demeaned by the process.

GIVING CRITICISM OR FEEDBACK

Giving criticism is an art. It is easy to offer suggestions or criticism when the other person asks. They have opened the door for you and given you permission. However, your rapport skills, the words you choose and how you say them are extremely important. That person's strong points need to honoured.

One suggestion is to ask the person for their own assessment of the situation. Likely they will have the answers already. What they are asking for is really some support from you. It is helpful to ask questions like, 'If there were no constraints of any kind, how would you sort out the problem?' or 'How can I/we help you to improve?' Once you have elicited a response, then give your own assessment of the issue or problem.

When you feel obliged to correct a situation where a person's behaviour or work is a problem, it is a bit more sticky. Ideally, you will be able to get them to see the problem by the way you approach it. However, this is not always possible and you have to tackle it head on. Talking these things over in a casual situation where you can build up a nice rapport is best. Boardroom or public bullying is not the way to generate self-esteem, quality work from your staff or to win you any Brownie points. It creates stress at all levels.

Stay away from personal language, ie, avoid words like 'you' and 'I' used in an accusing manner or as purely personal opinion. Here are some examples:

❑ 'In this company it is better to wear...'
❑ 'Is the project report complete as is?'
❑ 'The information on... might be valuable to the report'.

Bear in mind that the person you are addressing is still a fellow human being and his or her strengths are to be honoured.

Personal opinions are just that. You can choose to listen or not, depending on your own preferences and the circumstance. The personal opinion of your chief executive or director may be important. Listen. Ask appropriate questions and look at all your options. When people use words like, 'I do not like...' that is their prerogative. However, you do not have to take it personally. It is a stated opinion and basically it is their problem. Arguing with personal opinion is a fruitless task. It is better to allow them their opinion. You can respond by saying that it is not true for you. Our personal truths and perceptions are varied and different. You do not have to rescue the world or attend to all of its issues.

SCENARIOS

A: I do not like Jane Doe.
B: I do not know her well enough to have an opinion. She is certainly good at selling.

A: I like your hair better short.
B: That's interesting. Thanks for telling me.

HONESTY WITH WISDOM

Some people might say the scenario above was an example of being honest. However, the honesty in this case is an unsolicited personal opinion on the part of 'A'. 'B' is remaining positive by not debating the issue or arguing. Anyone is entitled to personal opinion. However, it has to be recognized as just that and not taken any further.

There are far more delicate and sensitive situations where it is necessary to be honest with another person. Redundancies, deaths, serious and life-threatening diseases are among the topics that arise in the professional arena. These situations are difficult for both parties. The seemingly easy, protective way out is to be brash, terse, do your best to show no feelings and say what has to be said quickly and remove yourself from the situation. In the long run this approach is an emotional disaster for both parties. Blatant honesty without wisdom can be extremely hurtful to the person on the other end of it and create a great deal of stress in the deliverer of the message. Sharing feelings is a way of creating rapport and gaining trust in this situation.

It is a skill to be able to say how you are feeling and empathize and be aware of the sensitivity of the other person at the same time. Honesty of fact and feelings is part of the message which must be appropriate, tactful and wise.

The next time you feel the need to be honest, ask yourself: if your honesty is purely a personal opinion; if your opinion has been solicited; whether the time is appropriate; or whether information is vital to the other person. After you have answered these questions you can choose to say something or remain silent. Sometimes it is wise to remain silent.

GIVING EFFECTIVE FEEDBACK IN GROUP SITUATIONS

Group situations provide many opportunities for feedback. If you are leading a meeting that includes your colleagues or staff there are a number of important issues which you might want to consider.

'Discovering' is a powerful learning experience; being told can be painful. An excellent manager has the ability to allow the staff member to discover for him or herself. Remember that the people with whom you are working are more vulnerable than they appear. It is easy to hurt people with careless comments or 'throw away remarks'. Although these remarks are not meant to hurt, they can be perceived to do that by a vulnerable person in a sensitive situation. Unfortunately, where personal change is concerned, comments are likely to be made more important than they are intended. Be aware of this and be willing to acknowledge the hurtfulness of the remark and apologize. It is not appropriate to be self-righteous in such circumstances.

First give a person the opportunity to say how she thought her performance satisfied her own goals. Check to see if her feelings and fears distorted her perceptions of the performance. Remember: 'How we look and how we think we look' are very different.

The most useful tool for self-discovery is the video. Even when a person is unwilling to acknowledge the need to change, he will see his behaviour and compare it to those around him. Quite often he will then implement the changes gradually as his 'secret'. When someone is too self-conscious or afraid of making a change, the video can offer convincing evidence that the change does not look or sound strange or over the top. When no video is available, mirroring or role-play can be used to allow the person to see her actions or behaviour.

Encourage positive and constructive responses from peers by setting an example in what you say, and the way you say it. Be ready to intervene to prevent a negative situation from arising.

Address issues and problems with something positive to do in place of the unwanted action or behaviour. Giving general directions like 'stand up straighter' will often create confusion. Clear directions for change are essential. When you do not know how to do this yourself, send that person to someone who does.

PERSONAL GUIDELINES FOR ACCEPTING AND GIVING CRITICISM

❑ Listen without internal dialogue and remain in rapport with the other person
❑ Use criticism and feedback as opportunities to learn more about yourself.

❏ First hear the other person out completely. Ask questions to bring out further specific information.

❏ Acknowledge the situation or problem. Others' perceptions are accurate as far as they know. Remain objective. Relate to the problem, not your emotions. Find a way to solve the situation rather than trying to change the other person.

❏ You can empathize with your critic without accepting the blame. A good way to resolve the situation is to acknowledge that there is a problem and clarify the issue by saying, 'Tell me what you would like instead' or 'Give me an example of what you would prefer.'

❏ When giving criticism, find something positive to say. People need guidelines. Find the good teacher in yourself by providing examples of what you want and give clear instructions.

❏ When you do not understand, ask for clarification. This saves a lot of time and misspent emotional energy.

8

THE ART OF PRESENTATION

According to opinion polls, one of the things that strike the most terror in men and women is to be asked to give a presentation. Most of the population become weak in the knees or self-conscious and suddenly feel the need to be perfect. In a millisecond their personal power is freely donated to an audience that is given credit for being able to see every wart, spot or error. The self-critic becomes the one giving the presentation and we forget that it is OK to be human. The person who was at home in her personal space suddenly becomes a stranger who is self-monitoring and apprehensive. Audiences do not expect perfection or a god in front of them, they come to hear your message. They deserve an enthusiastic, energetic person who is dedicated to, and congruent with, his or her message.

In a skilled speaker, presentation is a continuation of good communication skills and is visually, vocally and verbally congruent. It is concerned with rendering a message that is far more important than you personally. Every time you become aware of yourself or wonder what your audience is thinking, the message has been forgotten. Everything you say and do must match that message or it will become distorted in the minds of your audience. Anything like self-consciousness, gestures that have nothing to do with the message, pacing without a purpose, all create conflicting information. Ideally, the message and you are at one. When this happens, the speaker is spellbinding and captivating and the audience remembers.

WHAT MAKES A SPEAKER INTERESTING?

Spontaneity and complete dedication to the message play key parts in making someone interesting to hear. When we are 'at home' we tend to be spontaneous and uncritical about how we talk. Appropriate gestures, words, a voice that responds to the meaning and varying rhythms are all part of our communication. These are the attributes most needed in any kind of talk, from informal discussion with colleagues to boardroom presentations.

Faulty perceptions about what constitutes a presentation, and particularly a formal presentation, are at the root of 90 per cent of the problems relating to speaking in public. This causes people to lose confidence and to rely on memorization or reading their texts. Both of these are deadly. When you memorize a text you become excessively aware of going off script. The self-critic then takes over and it becomes difficult to be involved with the message. It is virtually impossible to react or respond to the needs of the audience with a memorized script. Unless you are a fine actor or have been specially coached, reading a speech is a poor way of being interesting. My clients find this out for themselves when we do the children's story exercise.

So many clients have told me that they have given presentations where they did not want to be there. My first response is, 'What makes you think the audience did not know that?' When the speaker is focused on the message, so is the audience. When your mind is elsewhere, so are the minds of your audience. It is your responsibility to make your audience want to hear more or to follow up on what you have said. They are not supposed to first attend a course on listening. You can stimulate them to pay attention.

BOREDOM FACTORS IN PRESENTATION

The listener who is not stimulated very quickly reverts to his own thought patterns and personal concerns. He is no longer there. Usually this person rationalizes that he can read your hand-out later. Anything about the presentation that establishes a repeated rhythmic pattern will put the audience to sleep – just as we use such patterns to go to sleep at night. In a way, it is just like counting sheep. Some of these patterns in a presentation are:

❑ every speaker sounding the same and using the same techniques;
❑ hand patterns that are tied to the rhythm of the words rather than the message;
❑ a controlled, monotonous voice;

❏ words that have no inherent rhythm or imagination behind them;
❏ slides that have too much information;
❏ speakers who appear to be unenthusiastic about their topics.

A number of boredom factors, which contribute to sleepy audience syndrome, are shown in the following sections.

The 'tell them' technique

While it is helpful for people to know what you are going to talk about, to give it in the form of a grocery list is an insult to the intelligence of your audience. Originally the concept of 'Tell them what you are going to tell them, tell them and then tell them what you told them' was probably a reasonable way to organize a talk. However, like most ideas, it has gradually become a kind of mechanized tool to create corpora.: or academic presentation clones. Nothing is worse than going to a business or scientific meeting where each presenter uses the same format, computer presentation templates, speech patterns, methods of delivery and professional jargon. Any time everything and everyone sounds the same and has similar rhythmic patterns, the audience will be lulled to sleep. People remember the presenters who are different. Paradoxically, those learning presentation skills are overly concerned with *not* being different.

Reading your talk

There are a few top-level directors of companies and politicians who are required to read public speeches as a matter of policy. The reason for this relates to media exposure and accuracy. Many of these directors are given coaching so that they can read as if they were speaking spontaneously. This takes rehearsal and practice.

For the rest of us who hurriedly scribble a presentation, discuss it only in our heads or count on a computer template for a quick way out, reading becomes a crutch. If you are not sure what it is like to be a recipient of the *'read'* presentation, have a colleague read part of a serious business paper to you. It is likely to have little or no spontaneity or normal speech quality in it.

Reading a presentation tends to inhibit the freedom and range of vocal expression, particularly when all the words and phrases are read at the same rhythm and pace. It becomes difficult to find the important points. Expressive reading is difficult without a great deal of rehearsal and planning. The children's story exercise in Chapter 5 is a way to rehearse a talk that must be read. However, such talks are rarely as spontaneous or effective as those that leave room to manoeuvre. Reading passages, quotes or specific data where accuracy is critical is acceptable. However, such material is best printed so members of your audience can review it in their own time without distraction. If they are busy looking at it while you are talking, you have lost them.

An excess of specific information

Managers, young teachers and others tend to want to tell an audience everything they know, leaving no space for the listener to absorb the material. Even when the listener has a focused mind, it is difficult for him to take in the vast amounts of information contained in excessive data, lists or complex graphs. This kind of presentation indicates that such a speaker is unsure of the message and therefore has tried to include everything he knows. Too much information causes indigestion, overwhelms the brain and frustrates the listener. The result is the mental loss of your audience.

I like to think of information like a fuel gauge – really more like a full or empty stomach. When you are on empty, you are uncomfortable. However, when you are full, at that moment you never want to see food again. The same is true of verbal or information overload. The fill-factor is best at about 75–80 per cent. That way your audience will have space to know whether they want more information or will want to go away and read your materials.

The apologetic presenter

You never need to apologize for being there or for giving a presentation. It is not part of your message and it sounds as if you are preparing the audience for a poor presentation. People are there to hear your message, not your excuses. We have far more expectations of ourselves than the audience does and it is usually the self-critic who is apologizing. The only time it is appropriate to apologize is when something unavoidable arises spontaneously during a talk.

ladies and gentlemen I would like to apologise for starting this presentation with an apology...

Um's and er's

Extraneous sounds occur because the speaker has a warped sense of time and feels the need to fill in the gaps in sound. For the presenter time goes slowly and any silence can seem an age. It is OK to be silent. Your audience will not go away. Those silent periods, usually lasting seconds, give your audience time to catch a breath and allow your information to sink in.

Many years ago I was having a terrible time making sense of the class notes from one particular course. I had thought that the professor was boring but I had not analysed the reason. The next class period I counted more than 40 um's and er's in 10 minutes. No wonder my lecture notes were a mess. It was difficult to find the beginnings and endings of sentences because they were chopped up with so many extraneous sounds. I tried to imagine what a foreign student would make of this language.

Apparently the new computer voice recognition systems are not understanding these extraneous sounds and they are creating havoc with dictation. Who would have thought that computers would improve our ability to speak?

In summary, repeated patterns that have no variety quickly become boring. You need to take a personal risk to give a presentation that is truly you rather than some habit or pattern you have memorized or learnt, consciously or unconsciously. If you do not want your audience to remember what you have said, why are you there?

APPROACHING PRESENTATION CREATIVELY

The creative approach to presentation offers variety, interest and substance to the listener and the speaker. Passing on useful information is similar to teaching. An outstanding teacher will offer knowledge in a way that the students want to listen and to participate. This can take many forms – anything from straight delivery to brainstorms and syndicate groups, group art work – I've even heard of a company composing and singing their own opera in a seminar on communication skills. Know that you have many, many options and dare to risk some of them. Organizing your approach and thoughts on the basis of wide-ranging choice will enable you to mix and match ideas spontaneously in your presentation.

Presentations become dull and lacking in spontaneity when they are treated like an essay or a piece of literature rather than a talk. The oral presentation model is not intended to be the same as the written model. We do not talk the way we write. When we do, it often sounds wooden and stilted. Written models are generally patterned on intellectual essays, school reports and/or scientific papers that are designed to be included in journals rather than given orally. It is not uncommon for written material given as an oral presentation to be repetitious, boring and to run over the time allotted.

We do not write and speak the same way and it is important that the two approaches are not confused. Think back to times you have discussed a work-related subject with friends and colleagues in comfortable, casual circumstances. Were you at a loss for words or a way to describe the information? And when they did not understand, probably you were able to describe issues in several different ways. However, the thought of giving a 'presentation' immediately conjures up concerns and thoughts of inadequacy. How is it that you are not inadequate with friends and barely functional with a perceived audience? The key to spontaneity and creativity is feeling at home in whatever space you occupy. Whatever you do, do not sit down and start to write a presentation without first going through the process outlined below.

How to play with your information and organize your material

Broaden your perspective first before you narrow it. Each profession has its own set of in-house jargon and preferred definitions and unfortunate assumptions are made regarding audience understanding of these. The best way to alleviate this problem is to pretend you have never heard of your topic before. Look up the keyword, and its original derivation, in a large dictionary and begin a mind-map of all the words that are given. Remember that this keyword is your topic, not necessarily the title of your talk. Do not edit out any words or ideas at this point. Accept what you see. If you use a word like 'management', be sure you look up the rootword, 'manage', as well. You may well come up with a few surprises and some thought-provoking definitions during this exercise.

After you have exhausted the dictionary definitions, think of all the associations, good, bad or otherwise, you might have with your chosen word. Add these to your mind map. Do not forget any sayings or phrases that come to mind. This part of the exercise is best done with a group, because each person will have his own associations and memories. You might also ask your spouse, children and colleagues what they think the word means. The diversity will astound you. The more you broaden your concept, the easier it is to come up with multiple ideas and options.

Now add any emotional words associated with your topic. While you may not think emotion is relevant to your topic, you will find that others have had pleasant or unpleasant experiences to share. In fact, many and varied emotions surround any topic.

At this point you will have a page full of words. If you wish to group them into major headings or topics, do so. You may have a subject that contains several modifying words, eg, 'group financial management'. Think of ways these words might modify your main topic. Include the most important of these words now. However, do not start to plan your talk yet. Before beginning to work on your talk, there are some questions that need to be answered.

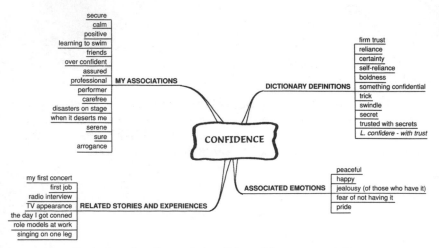

Brainstorming the topic 'confidence' for a presentation

Ask yourself the following questions before preparing your presentation:

Q: *What one thing do I want my audience to remember?*

Note: This answer is informed also by your knowledge of your audience, who they are and why they are there.

A: The answer to this question can be a fact, a value, a concept or the creation of trust or credibility for you or your company. Unless you have an answer, you will not have a focus for your presentation.

Q: *How much can people remember?*

A: You do not want to leave them with information overload and indigestion. If you have five minutes, one main point is all you can make. The maximum for any talk is five major headings – and still only one focus.

Q: *How clear are my data?*

A: While you live with your data all the time, you cannot expect an audience to decipher them as quickly as you. Keep charts and graphs simple and key items well marked or ˥loured. Anything complex needs to be put on a special ˥d-out.

Q: *How do I show my main point(s) on a slide or overhead?*

Note: Remember that most people store information in pictures and are visual. Therefore a simple picture or a cartoon is very helpful.

A: Make sure that your important items can be seen a split second after a slide is shown. If your audience has to look to find or follow the information, they will not hear what you are saying. In other words, make points blatantly obvious.

Q: *Would a simple one-page hand-out be useful?*

A: It is much easier to go away with one page than a wad of paper and far less daunting. Using your slides as hand-outs saves time but they are more likely to wind up in the bin. More will be said about this later.

Q: *What approach will I take?*

A: This will be dependent on the size of the group, the topic and the atmosphere you wish to create. There are numerous options available: discussion, brainstorm, syndicates. With a large group you can get them to interact with each other for a short time. I have seen it done with as many as 800. For example, pose a question and give your audience three minutes to discuss it with those nearby. It will start them thinking and they will be ready to listen to your thoughts on the subject.

Q: *What are my personal options? Is it appropriate for me to stand? Or sit?*

A: For small groups, I suggest that you sit. Be one of them and you will establish a better rapport. You can get up to write on a flipchart or change a slide when necessary.

Know whether you want to use a lectern or a microphone. Your comfort and ease during the presentation are important. Do not be afraid to ask for what you want.

Having answered the above questions, you are now ready to begin to organize the ideas and text of your presentation. In fact, much of your work will have been done by following the process I have outlined.

Introduction

Look at the words on your mind-map. Are there any stories, experiences, or real life situations that would serve as a good introduction? The introduction serves only one purpose – to get your audience interested in hearing what else you have to say and to establish the focus on your issue or topic. Your introduction can be varied infinitely. It can be a story, incident from work or a short, one word brainstorm that sets the stage for what comes next. You may choose on the day to change your introduction. When you have done the preparation above, you will be able to make the change easily.

The introduction is the time to create 'common ground'. You create common ground by relating first to the human beings in the audience. Then you present *people* your information – not *information* to the people. Think for a moment where your emphasis is. Is it on data and facts or is it on your audience and their needs?

CASE STUDY

A large company was holding seminars on a new software program for its information technology (IT) staff. The presenter wanted the staff to grasp some basic concepts related to a change in work practices. The company had changed from a six- to a seven-day work week and this affected the way information was being downloaded on the computers. There was now no day for downloading.

The title of the presenter's talk was 'Triggers and Batches'. I sent him to look up the word 'batches' in a dictionary. He returned laughing and said that the definition was perfect for his concept. He said that they could no longer put batches of material in the computer but now had to feed it in small bits over each day – much like the Pizza Hut conveyor belt style of fulfilling specific orders for pizzas. For his introduction he created a cartoon of a baker putting in a batch of loaves and a conveyor belt full of pizzas. Even though he was talking to very knowledgeable IT staff, they immediately got the picture because of their own experiences with something as common as baking bread or making pizzas. They did not forget his message – he talked first to humans, then to the computer designers.

SOME PITFALLS AND WORDS TO AVOID IN INTRODUCTIONS:

'I would like to talk to you…' (just do it)
'I am going to talk about…' (again, just do it)
'I hope you will…' (weakens)
Jokes that have nothing to do with the topic.
Insincere greetings. When you say, 'Good morning, ladies and gentlemen, etc', you must mean it. Look at your audience, not your notes, when you include a greeting and mentally give them time to reply. Those words need a pause afterwards. Do not just launch into your talk without a break.

Tip: To create a pause you can repeat your greeting silently to yourself.

Body of the talk

Now that you have people interested, give them specific information and detail. Return to your mind-map for the organization of appropriate concepts and headings. I had one client who organized his presentation by having a picture for each main heading. He then gave specific information by talking about the various elements in each picture.

There is a variety of ways of presenting the body of your talk: in-depth brainstorming as a group or in a syndicate, questions and answers specific to the issues you want discussed, role-plays, mini-dramas or a simple, direct presentation. You must decide whether you wish to talk or facilitate. The more you are able to allow your audience to take part, the more they will own the topic. However, facilitation needs careful planning and the ability to respond quickly and think on your feet. It demands flexibility and spontaneity.

Be adaptable enough to be able to shorten, lengthen or rearrange the order of your points. Their survival and yours are not dependent on getting every word that you have planned. Be observant of the needs of your audience and change the pace or direction when necessary.

Summary

This section can be powerful, persuasive or gentle, depending on the message you choose to deliver. It is useful to include benefits and emotional comparisons like, 'People who manage this way are less frustrated and enjoy their work', 'Employees who follow these guidelines will save themselves time and energy and the company will see a higher profit', 'The way to keep your customers happy is to...', etc. You may repeat your main message. For example, 'If you take only one idea away with you today, I would like it to be...'

PRESENTATION TOOLS

After you have decided on the primary message and purpose of your presentation, you can make some choices about how to present the material. This is determined somewhat by the size of your audience, the kind of atmosphere you wish to create (casual, serious, etc), the available equipment, seating and platform arrangements. Ask questions about these things ahead of time so that there are no unpleasant surprises. Do not be afraid to request the arrangements you want. Too many times the organizers of presentation events make assumptions about how they are given. For example, many seminars are set up around big tables with no space left to manoeuvre chairs. If you are planning group interaction, this can be disastrous.

When you know your material well, do it with few or no notes. You may want to have a very brief one-page outline to keep you on track. Ideally, the introduction will be completely spontaneous. For the rest of your information you may use notes, cards, speak to your slides or pictures. Make sure you get to a presentation or seminar early to check the set-up, your slides, overhead, proper pens, etc. More importantly, you want to get a feel for the space and make it your home.

Effective use of slides

Putting important points on a slide or overhead is useful. The 'visual' majority of your audience will appreciate this. Wherever possible, think in pictures. Out of this may come some clever ways to put across your ideas. Unfortunately, the common practice is to put words and complicated graphs on slides. Simplicity is the key.

Some presenters use their slides as keynotes for memory. This is acceptable as long as each word and sentence is *not* read to the audience. They can read for themselves. It is better for you to explain why those points are there and the specific information related to them. The objective is to maintain a spontaneous, flexible and comfortable format. Trust your knowledge; you do not need to read the slides.

Hand-outs made from slides

It is the custom to reproduce slide materials and use them as hand-outs. Hand-outs of slides are more useful to the presenter than the audience. Often they are used, quite legitimately, as reminders for the speaker and to highlight main points for the

EFFECTIVE USE OF SLIDES...

audience. Sometimes they provide something to do for a bored audience. However, more often than not, people use them as an easy short cut and the listener is left with a wad of paper that makes no sense later. It is far better to condense the material into one or two pages of reminders. This means you have to rethink your information and make it useful for the audience rather than yourself.

INTERACTIVE PRESENTATION AND FACILITATION

The skill of interactive presentation lies in making it easy for your audience to respond. The value of interaction is that it gives your audience the responsibility of doing some work and for thinking for themselves. Also they are more likely to own or share the outcome. It is a form of acknowledgement for you to allow them to have their say. Many decisions are made without consulting staff. This is a way to include them in both planning and decisions.

Brainstorming

When you want to find out quickly what the group is thinking, use a one-word brainstorm. This can be done with small or large groups. There are a number of ways to do this.

Note: How you word your question(s) for the brainstorm is extremely important. The more specific your question, the more specific the answer you will receive.

The following is an example of a question that will elicit a short response without lengthy statements: What is the first word that comes to mind when I say the word 'manage'? This kind of one-word response is useful when you want to get a quick picture of the thinking of your group. It takes no time and can provide a good introduction or a provocative discussion later. I have seen this used in a group of over 200 people.

In this case, a small piece of paper was placed on the chairs of the participants before the talk began. During the opening remarks they were asked to write the word that arose when the term 'alliance' was mentioned. The papers were then passed to the end of the rows, collated and put up for the audience to see in a later part of the presentation. The positive associations were put on one side, the negative on the other. The sense of the group reaction to the term was readily apparent.

During a brainstorming session it is important that you include every person and accept every word offered. You can also add your own. If they do not come up with one of your keywords, put theirs up first and then suggest the one word they did not think of, or ask permission to add yours. You are in charge of the discussion, so you can choose the words that are key to your message to move further into your presentation.

Syndicate or Breakout groups

Done well, syndicate groups will make your presentation for you. Sometimes it is nice to let them do all the work. Your job is to oversee, accept what they have to offer and shape the message. This takes careful and thoughtful planning. Getting the response you want will depend directly on the way you present the questions or issues and your clarity about the outcome you want.

Issues or questions that are too general will generate too many ideas and will lack focus. For example, 'What are the problems in your department relating to supply management?' This question could generate many answers, a lot of negativity and no steps to a solution. A better way of presenting the issue is, 'What are the three main issues relating to "supply management" in your department? What is working well at the moment? What problem areas need immediate focus? Come up with three ways of solving these areas.'

A WORD ABOUT SCIENTIFIC OR TECHNICAL PAPERS

It is common to have 10 to 20 minutes to present material at conferences. This material usually is a report of research and/or highly specific findings. It is the fashion to use the paper to be submitted for publication as the basis of the oral presentation. Unfortunately this is often boring, filled with excess information, and the real excitement and passion about the research is omitted.

Focus your attention on the one thing you would like your audience to take away from your presentation. When speakers are intent on delivering vast amounts of information, it leads to excess material being crammed into a short period of time and a speaker who talks too quickly and overrunning the time allotted. When in doubt, say less.

Data and specific lists are best shown as simple graphs and summarized during your talk. After an audience has heard six speakers pour out technological data and jargon in a period of an hour and a half, they are more than saturated. People cannot retain this detail in their heads, therefore create hand-outs that can be read at their leisure. Your job is to create so much interest that each person will want to go away and read them.

Your audience does not need to know everything that you have learnt in order to present the paper. You are there because you have something to offer from your perspective. Others may be knowledgeable in your field. However, they will not know the information in the way that you do.

Presenters who dare to be different have presentations that are remembered. When there are 'assembly-line' type talks at conferences, they all begin to sound the same. This puts an audience to sleep quickly. It is important to be different (and interesting) in this situation. It is your responsibility to keep the audience awake.

Share your information and your enthusiasm with your audience. Speak to them as if they were friends in your home. Scientific and technical presentations can be made exciting, interesting and fun.

PRESENTATIONS AS A PART OF A JOB INTERVIEW

It is common for interviewees to have to give a short presentation. Do not forget that in the last instance, it is your choice as to whether you want that job. In your interview and presentation you will wish to know if you want to work with these people and this company. Sometime during the interview, make sure that you find out where they want the company or section to go and what are the current problems. This will assist you in analysing their needs and wishes and enable you to speak specifically to these during your presentation.

TIMING YOUR TALK

Experienced speakers and classroom teachers know how to keep to a schedule when presenting. They have learned over time just how much time they need for the amount of information they wish to relay. Inexperienced speakers can find timing difficult. Timing your talk by speaking it or reading it aloud is an essential part of your preparation.

If you are reading your presentation, you can easily time it. A single-spaced page of text read at a reasonable pace will take approximately two-and-a-half to three minutes. Taking less time will indicate to you that you are reading too fast.

While speaking with notes or to slides is more spontaneous, it is less easy to time. However, as a rough guideline, a twenty minute talk should have about five to seven slides and no more than four main points. I once watched in horror as a speaker, who had been given strict instructions to give a twenty minute talk, appeared with about forty overheads. She spoke for well over an hour, oblivious to the fact that there were other speakers.

While most audiences will love you if you finish your presentation early, the opposite may happen if you run over. When your presentation goes over your allotted time, you become extremely unpopular with your audience, the next speaker and the organizers of the seminar. Even if you think that every word you have prepared needs to be delivered, your audience does not. They have lost interest and concentration at this point. It is much better to stop short, do a quick summary of the material you are currently presenting and cut to the end of your presentation.

When you are unsure of your timing or afraid that you will go over, ask a friend or colleague in the audience or the person in charge of the event to signal to you when you have five minutes remaining. That way, you will not be surprised or be caught without enough time to close your presentation in a logical way.

GIVING YOUR PRESENTATION

Presenting yourself well and receiving feedback and acknowledgement from your audience is an exhilarating experience. First-time actors and singers, and sometimes teachers, find themselves on a real high when they experience the wave of energy that comes from the audience. Speakers who have the same experience grow to love the interaction with audiences, large or small.

To present well, you need to take some concepts and tools from earlier chapters. The most important one is the concept of personal space. Make sure that you have visualized yourself doing well and feeling 'at home' as you plan your presentation and immediately preceding it. Remember that you can expand your space to include any size audience or room. Welcome the audience into your home.

Think of your centre as being located between your pubic bone and your navel. Breathe in and out of that area and support your voice from there. If you are using a microphone, remember that it is there purely to magnify the sound you put into it. Using a microphone is not an excuse to produce a flimsy, unsupported voice.

Just before you speak, make sure you sit quietly with both feet firmly on the floor, breathing deeply and observing what is happening around you. Do not memorize your opening lines. Focus on the one thing you want the audience to take away from

your talk. Remember that as long as you are fully focused on your message, so is your audience. The minute your mind begins to worry, become self-conscious or lose focus, the audience focuses on you, not your message.

While you are speaking, plant your feet on the floor. Grounding is important for your energy, nerves and voice. Move only with a purpose, ie to get to the slides, flipchart, talk to someone specifically. Mindless pacing uses your brain power for movement rather than the message. The message is at its best and effective when you are integrated visually, vocally and textually.

If you should lose track of where you are or make a mistake, pause for a moment, take a deep breath and let your audience know what has happened. They are sympathetic and probably aware that something is causing discomfort. Your acknowledgement of the situation will help put you and your audience at ease.

Using your hands

We use our hands comfortably and naturally in everyday life. However, when we are told to keep them still, we tend to develop extraneous twitches of hands, heads, shoulders, hips and feet as substitutes for using them in a talk. People who live whole days, weeks and months without thinking once about what to do with their hands become paranoid about them when faced with a presentation. Some of this paranoia has been given to them by well-meaning consultants who have told them to keep their hands still.

Hands are part of the visual aspects of your presentation. As long as they move in tandem with the messages and words you are using, they are fine. One purpose of the children's story exercise is to show you ways of using your hands effectively. Some people have been taught to fold their hands in front in the 'fig-leaf' or 'crotch' position. (Wherever you keep your

hands stationary will call attention to that part of the body.) You choose what you would like to emphasize. Hands look perfectly normal hanging by your sides or using them expressively and with purpose. Frozen-hand positions look far more awkward than using them to express the message. If you are worried about this, record your presentation on video so you can see for yourself.

Think of your presentation as a way of sharing your information with your audience. You are not talking at people or trying to give them 'information indigestion'. No talk, about any subject, ever has to be indigestible or boring.

WHAT IF ...?

Presentations are rarely, if ever, perfect. Knowing this is the first step to remaining centred when something does go amiss. It is worth considering some of the things that might create a momentary panic and cause you to lose confidence during a talk.

Just before you get up to speak you discover you are wearing mismatched socks

The first thing you need to know is that you will probably be the only one in the whole auditorium or room that knows it. When you are involved completely and totally in your presentation, your audience will be focused on that as well. However, when a speaker is boring, members of an audience will begin to look around for something to interest them. It could well be your socks.

CASE STUDY

A number of years ago I needed some shoes to wear with the gown I was wearing for a concert (solo) I was to give. Hastily, I ran into the shoe shop and tried on several pairs of shoes. My choice came down to two almost identical pairs. The only difference was that one

---

pair had slightly higher heels. I chose the pair with the lower heels. They were duly boxed and handed to me. The night of the concert I dressed backstage and put my shoes on last. Surprise! The sales-person at the shoe shop had put in a mixed pair of shoes – one each of the different heel heights. There was no choice except to use them, smile and walk on stage as if my legs were even. Fortunately, there was only a few millimetres difference in the size, and even more fortunately there were not two right shoes in the box, and thank God for the long dress.

I sang the concert with no mishaps, physically or musically, and was relieved when the end arrived. In talking with friends and concert-goers later, I found that not a single person had noticed the difference in my shoes. Thankfully, they had all been occupied with the music instead.

Moral: Always double check all the clothing you plan to wear the day before as well as on the day of your presentation.

You lose your place

This is more of an issue when you read a speech. Make sure you have the text in large print with adequate line spacing. If you do find yourself lost, take a deep breath, stop to find your place and continue. Remember that time is going slowly for you and fast for your audience. They are most likely to perceive your momentary stop as a pause and welcome the chance to catch up with you.

Today, the practice of using slides, overheads or note cards tends to keep the speaker from getting lost as well as staying on track. If you are worried about straying from your subject, give yourself a time for each part of your talk and check your watch periodically to make sure you are where you planned to be. If you do lose your place or skip something you wanted to say, simply let the audience know what you have done and backtrack to that item.

There is a slide in the wrong place

It does not matter whether you placed it in the wrong place, put it in upside down or whether the technician did it. Do not bother to try to place blame but simply explain what has happened and correct it if possible within a short time. It is maddening for the audience and for you if technical problems appear to take a great deal of time to correct. If the slide cannot be moved easily, you will have to flip back and forth until you have finished speaking about that part of your presentation.

There is a problem with the visual aids, no slide or overhead projector

When Murphy's law is in full force, there is little you can do except improvise. However, when in doubt, err on the side of simplicity. Do not attempt to read large amounts of data to an audience. Instead describe the picture you were planning to show or tell a story around the data. If the visual information or picture was critical to your presentation, ask the members of your audience to draw or outline how they might see this picture. In other words turn the situation around and get your audience to do the work. Your presentation may be far more spontaneous and better than you planned.

CASE HISTORY

I once was told at the last minute that I had no slide projector for an anatomy lecture on the larynx. Anatomy is difficult without pictures and I was not good at drawing the structures. What followed was one of the best classes I had ever given. I asked the class to get out their anatomy books and together we all made models of the larynx out of notebook paper, tape and staples. They never forgot the cartilages of the larynx.

There is no microphone

In this case remember that you have included the whole audience in your personal space. It will then be easier to fill that space with your voice. You will need to support your voice with the muscles of the abdomen so you will be much more physically active. Ask people in different areas of the room or auditorium to let you know when they cannot understand or hear you. And lastly, think of yourself as an actor or actress on a large stage.

It's my first time speaking in public

Giving a first performance of any kind is likely to be nerve racking. If you are totally calm, you will probably make history as being the first ever to be so. The best way to allay fear is to practice a lot and visualize yourself being at ease on the day. Practise talking aloud to yourself in front of a mirror and talk about your subject with willing friends and colleagues.

If your mind goes blank, take a deep breath and slowly check your notes. Time will be going incredibly slowly for you so you will feel you are taking hours when it is really only seconds. No audience I know has ever left in mid-sentence.

Quiet shaking hands by placing them firmly on the podium; however, do not grip so tightly that your hands turn white. The best way to alleviate nervous hands and mannerisms is to use your hands meaningfully. Reread the children's story exercise and the section above on hands.

Remember you are speaking because you are sharing your knowledge. You would not be there if the subject matter were not part of your professional expertise or within your scope of knowledge.

There is a question I cannot answer

Honesty is best. When you do not know the answer to a question, say so. Bluffing your way through invites far more embarrassment than saying you do not know. Offer to find out the answer or to send that person to someone who is knowledgeable in that area. Remember you are not God and being human is OK.

When the question is irrelevant, quickly find a nice way to ask that person how it applies to the information in your talk. If she can apply it, clarify the question. If she cannot, tell her that you will be happy to discuss it with her later. Make a point to see her after the talk so she will not feel neglected.

A person tries to take over your talk by making a long statement

There are some people who feel a need to let an audience know about their personal beliefs and knowledge – even to take the opportunity to show off. They do not have a question but begin to state a personal opinion and possibly start a debate. When the statement appears to be inappropriate or too long, it is best to find the earliest opportunity to interrupt nicely. As the speaker, you have every right to ask such a person if he is asking a question or making a statement. He will then need to define what he is doing. You can suggest to him that this time is set aside for questions. Perhaps you could meet him afterwards and discuss his point.

If his point is valid and you feel comfortable with letting him talk, then do so. However, it is your time and you must take charge of it. Once his main point has been made, I recommend you summarize his point and move on.

You have a misguided supporter

Occasionally a friend will try to help you out and add information that is not appropriate or is off the point. Simply thank them for their point and continue your presentation.

There are unwanted interruptions or hecklers

This is an unlikely situation in the normal presentation setting.

However, interruptions and hecklers can appear in debates and in political and controversial situations. You must be careful to gauge the situation and the people. If the interference is mostly innocent fun, you can usually stop it by inviting those people to demonstrate or share what they were discussing with the whole group. Most of the time they are embarrassed and stop immediately.

In the first instance of heckling, politely ignore it and continue your talk. However, if it becomes serious you may need to ask for help from the organizers of the event. I had a friend who often spoke on controversial subjects and knew she would be heckled or shouted down. I suggested that she put her information on slides or overheads and then it would not matter if she could not be heard. This is an extreme case and it would occur rarely.

People get restless

When people become restless in a talk it can be for a number of reasons. For the insecure speaker, it is easiest to think that you are being boring. That is a possibility. However, when people have been sitting for long periods of time listening to a number of speakers, it is normal. When you notice restlessness, there are a number of things you can do to change the energy: 1) Get everyone to stand up and stretch; 2) Ask them a question; 3) Get them to share information about the topic with the person sitting beside them; 4) Do a quick brainstorm; 5) Take a five minute break. Rather than just giving information, find a way to get your audience to give it to you.

There is little response to questions you ask

When you get little response to your questions, first rephrase them in case they have not been understood. If there is still no response, give them a question and ask them to share answers with the people near them. Sometimes members of an audience are unwilling to answer a question in public where they might seem inadequate. This is particularly true with young people and meetings where junior staff and senior executives are both in attendance. They will happily talk with each other, but are not forthcoming in addressing the whole group. Very rarely is the audience, or anyone in it, your enemy. However, this is often the perception. When you expect an audience, or anyone else for that matter, to be an enemy, you are setting up a negative situation that invites negative reaction. Make friends with your audience, respect them and their knowledge, speak positively about your subject and be a good listener when someone takes issue with what you have said. Involve your audience in the process by asking them questions and making them think. This is the best way for information to be shared and owned by everyone.

SUMMARY

Presentation is an art when you:

❑ are yourself – your best self – as if the audience is sitting and listening to you in your own living room;
❑ are gracious – be the host or hostess to your audience – as if you are offering something valuable to each person without being pretentious;
❑ speak with enthusiasm – show your interest and passion in the subject and allow the audience to be included in your personal relationship with the topic;
❑ create space for the audience to absorb and understand what you are saying. They need time to see, hear and experience the information you are giving them;
❑ keep your information simple – put complicated subject matter in simple form on hand-outs, where they will have a chance to read it over and over when they do not understand it or wish to think about it more carefully.

Note: Absorbing oral information is difficult, so be considerate of your audience when planning your presentation. Remember the 'fuel' gauge.

❏ allow your audience to participate in some way – do not do the thinking for your audience. They need active participation if they are to get anything out of your talk. Do not let them become 'couch potatoes' when you speak – this applies to both large and small group presentations;

❏ prepare your presentation by talking it over with a number of people first. Find out what makes sense to other people, friends and colleagues. Talking about your material clarifies it in your own mind and allows you to know when you are too complicated. You may find what you thought was clear in your mind sounds disorganized when stated aloud.

Action planning and summary

ACTION PLANNING

Choose one thing only to work on for a day or a week, if necessary. Remind yourself of the thing you wish to change by leaving Post-it notes in obvious places such as your bathroom mirror, the dashboard of the car, your desk, by the telephone, the top of

our lecture or presentation notes or any place where your eyes naturally fall during the day. These notes may contain a word, a simple phrase or a symbol such as an arrow for 'tall'. Your concentration has to be on your work, so the notes will serve as polite reminders in the off-moments.

More is not necessarily better. So engage in any of the exercises such as those on posture, voice, awareness, 180-degree vision, listening or remaining still for three minutes. Write yourself notes to use as reminders for the rest of the day.

CREATE A THREE-TIERED ACTION PLAN

1. First outline, mind-map, or list an overall picture of how you would like to be perceived or see yourself in five years.

❑ What personal characteristics would you like to have?
❑ Which values are dear to you?
❑ What role would you like to have in your profession?
❑ What characteristics, personal and professional, would you consider ideal for someone in that role?
❑ Which of these do you have now?

2. Next make a list of all the things you do best. This can include anything from your professional skills to your hobbies – even DIY or reading to your children. Do not be modest. This is a list for you.

❑ If you could do anything you wanted to do professionally, what would it be?
❑ What further skills would you like to have to accomplish this?
❑ List the simplest, first steps you can take towards accomplishing your goals.

3. Create a list of priorities gathered from the answers to the questions above.

❑ Determine the easiest possible way to begin.
❑ What small things can you begin to practise, think or do now?
❑ Mark a start-time in your diary.

SUMMARY

Personal power is taking charge of how you feel about your life and knowing that you have choices in how you lead it. All the chapters in this book have been dedicated to helping you see and understand some of the choices you have. You do have the choice and the ability to change. It is not dependent on anyone else around you.

As mentioned earlier, many of our problems lie in our perceptions. Yes, they have been carefully taught in some instances. When we are taught only one way or one answer for something, it makes everything else seem wrong. After years of such thinking, it is difficult to look afresh at what we do and how we are. We become full of iron-bound ideas and change with difficulty. Personal power is given away to these preconceptions and misconceptions.

Such preconceptions and lack of sensitivity are large obstacles to understanding ourselves and those around us. We begin to define who we are by what we do and create identity problems. In this instance, personal power has been given away to what we do. Emphasis on work and earning power can cause confusion as to who we are and what our motivations for going to work are.

You cannot require another person to take on the changes you are making. They will have a different list. We only make changes when we are ready. The pieces of the puzzle fit only when other pieces are in place. The responsibility and choice are purely yours for yourself – not anyone else – not the world.

WAYS OF MAINTAINING YOUR PERSONAL POWER

❑ Make sure you do one thing each week that is special to you. You are worth it! Have a massage, engage in a sport or hobby, go to an art class or sing.
❑ Be aware of maintaining a dynamic rather than a static posture. Do not drag yourself down.

❑ Schedule, and adhere to, short periods of quiet time. These periods can be as short as three minutes. You are in charge of your time.

❑ Remember to acknowledge those around you. You are never too busy to see, smile or speak to those near you.

❑ Enjoy and value your friends and colleagues. Allow them their own opinions. You can do your best when you allow others to do theirs.

❑ Take a serious look at your values and the way in which they relate to your everyday life and work. It is virtually impossible to work with a personal value system which does not match the one that exists in your job. When this mismatch of values occurs, it depletes your energy.

❑ Know that your self-worth and self-esteem are not attached to your wealth, position or those with whom you associate. Self-worth comes from self-knowledge, self-respect and self-acceptance.

❑ Want to be where you are at all times.

USING THESE TOOLS WISELY

This book is full of tools for your personal development. You know what you want and need. You can choose few or many of these tools that you feel will help you. The desire to change will cause your 'computer' to begin to program itself.

Enjoy the process of growth. Laugh at yourself. Share the experiences, happy, sad or otherwise, and the doing of these exercises with your family and friends. Make presence and personal power into a community endeavour. These are not secret attainments only for the privileged. They are available to everyone. The by-products of your efforts will lead to increased trust in yourself and greater confidence.

Confidence – from *confidere* – with full trust.

FURTHER READING

Adams, S (1997) *The Dilbert Principle*, Boxtree, London

Argyle *et al.* (1970) in *British Journal of Social and Clinical Psychology* Vol. 9, pp. 222–31

Goleman, D (1996) *Emotional Intelligence*, Bloomsbury, London

Laborde, G (1987) *Influencing with Integrity, Management Skills for Communication and Negotiation*, Syntony Publishing, Palo Alto, California

Langer, E (1998) *The Power of Mindful Learning*, Addison Wesley, Reading, Massachusetts

Lundin, W and Lundin, K (1998) *When Smart People Work for Dumb Bosses, How to Survive in a Crazy and Dysfunctional Workplace*, McGraw-Hill, New York

Matthews, A (1988) *Being Happy*, Media Masters, Singapore

Matthews, A (1990) *Making Friends*, Media Masters, Singapore

Rees, F (1998) *The Facilitator Excellence Handbook, Helping People Work Creatively and Productively Together*, Jossey-Bass, San Francisco

Urech, E (1997) *Speaking Globally, How to Make Effective Presentations Across International and Cultural Boundaries*, Kogan Page, London

Whyte, D (1996) *The Heart Aroused: Poetry and the Preservation of the Soul in Corporate America*, Doubleday, New York

Further information about Meribeth Bunch's work in business and the performing arts, seminars, lectures and publications can be found on the Internet at: www.creating-confidence.com